Writing and Unrecognized Academic Labor

Writing and Unrecognized Academic Labor acknowledges that much of the work we do to sustain the academy remains without recognition. It demonstrates that it is not only published work that influences development and innovation in scholarship.

The book rethinks the "publish or perish" system to show that good, unrecognized work is a vital part of scaffolding the growth of the academy and individual academic careers. It takes openness and transparency as a blueprint to outline plans for not only producing but also reimagining key markers of academic life, such as dissertations without anxieties of influence, conferences without directors, journals without gatekeepers, large-sample peer review, and teaching and learning beyond the university discourse.

A sustainable community model of academic life should have belonged to each of us from the start. Author James Salvo shows us that "nothing will be lost when everything is given away. Thus, we ought to share fearlessly." This book is suitable for all graduate students and researchers in qualitative inquiry and across disciplines who seek a new model for the value of their work.

James M. Salvo is a lecturer in the College of Education at Wayne State University, USA.

Developing Traditions in Qualitative Inquiry
Series Editors: Jasmine Brooke Ulmer and James Salvo
Wayne State University

The Developing Traditions in Qualitative Inquiry series invites scholars to share novel and innovative work in accessible ways, ways such that others might discover their own paths, too. In acknowledging who and what have respectively influenced our work along the way, this series encourages thoughtful engagements with approaches to inquiry – ones that are situated within ongoing scholarly conversations. Neither stuck in tradition nor unaware of it, volumes make new scholarly contributions to qualitative inquiry that attend to what's shared across disciplines and methodological approaches. By design, qualitative inquiry is a tradition of innovation in and of itself, one aimed at the target of justice.

From multiple perspectives and positionalities, concise volumes in this series (20,000 to 50,000 words) strengthen and grow the qualitative community by developing inquiry traditions as they should be developed: inclusively, diversely, and together.

For more information about the series or proposal guidelines, please write the Series Editors at jasmine.ulmer@wayne.edu and salvo@wayne.edu.

Other volumes in this series include:

Shared and Collaborative Practice in Qualitative Inquiry
Tiny Revolutions
Jasmine Brooke Ulmer

Writing and Unrecognized Academic Labor
The Rejected Manuscript
James M. Salvo

For a full list of titles in this series, please visit www.routledge.com/ Developing-Traditions-in-Qualitative-Inquiry/book-series/DTQI

Writing and Unrecognized Academic Labor
The Rejected Manuscript

James M. Salvo

LONDON AND NEW YORK

First published 2021
by Routledge
2 Park Square, Milton Park, Abingdon, Oxon OX14 4RN

and by Routledge
52 Vanderbilt Avenue, New York, NY 10017

Routledge is an imprint of the Taylor & Francis Group, an informa business

© 2021 James M. Salvo

The right of James M. Salvo to be identified as the author of this work has been asserted in accordance with sections 77 and 78 of the Copyright, Designs and Patents Act 1988.

All rights reserved. No part of this book may be reprinted or reproduced or utilised in any form or by any electronic, mechanical, or other means, now known or hereafter invented, including photocopying and recording, or in any information storage or retrieval system, without permission in writing from the publishers.

Trademark notice: Product or corporate names may be trademarks or registered trademarks, and are used only for identification and explanation without intent to infringe.

British Library Cataloguing-in-Publication Data
A catalogue record for this book is available from the British Library

Library of Congress Cataloging-in-Publication Data
A catalog record for this book has been requested

ISBN: 978-0-367-35582-1 (hbk)
ISBN: 978-0-429-34045-1 (ebk)

Typeset in Times New Roman
by Apex CoVantage, LLC

To Boo Boo, Lover of Wildflowers

Contents

	Preface: continuing traditions	viii
1	Giving it away from the start	1
2	Dissertations	11
3	Conferences	20
4	Online media, social or otherwise	28
5	Reviewing	34
6	Teaching	42
	Works cited	49
	Index	51

Preface: continuing traditions

Back in the early 1990s when I was minoring in women's studies – no major was available, so I redeclared it to be English – we read a particularly difficult book, at that time new, by Judith Butler. It introduced me to both feminist theory and poststructural philosophy. Before then, I had only considered myself to be a Marxist. I remember talking to my friends Cass and Jerry – it was Cass, by the way, who encouraged me to go into my minor – about whether we'd ever see any changes in our lifetime regarding all the good stuff we read in *Gender Trouble*. I recall very clearly that I was pessimistic. Today, I'm very glad to have been proved wrong.

If one remembers the 1990s, one knows that we've nicely come a long way. True, not all the way, but far. If one doesn't remember the 1990s, maybe watch the show *Friends*, try not to cringe as a feminist, and realize that all that was considered to be, at the time, okay. In a way, as difficult as *Gender Trouble* had been to understand, we might say that the discussion in small university circles – discussions like those that took place between Cass, Jerry, and me – moved beyond the university discourse and made things better in the world. As educators, I don't think we're taking too much credit for ourselves if we think such things in general. Education, we know, makes a difference.

But if you think a little further back along the chain of causality, you know that *Gender Trouble* wouldn't be possible were it not for William Germano, who was the publishing director at Routledge. It was under Germano that *Gender Trouble* was published. Under Germano, we also get other feminist and philosophical classics that contributed to the discussion. Unpacking my library and handling – I still think this should be *tactile* and not *tactical* – some classics from my bookshelf, I see that many of my favorite books had been from Germano-era Routledge. Look, here's *The Spivak Reader*, and oh, Diana Fuss's *Essentially Speaking*. And here, too, is something from Cornel West.

At any rate, if Judith Butler may have started a conversation that changed the world for the better, and you don't have any of that without Germano's support, yet many people are unfamiliar with his name because those books don't bear his signature, then we really ought to recognize his unrecognized academic work. Thinking toward our qualitative corner, we don't have many important books that we have without Mitch Allen. Today, because she's almost single-handedly continuing the tradition, we don't have the important new works that we do without Hannah Shakespeare at Routledge.[1]

***

And now because I'm having a bit of uncontrollable nostalgia about my early days of study, let's blow off some dust and have a peek inside some of those books I just mentioned. I like to read. Read, read, read, we're told by Bettie St.Pierre. Reading is important, but often unrecognized academic work. They really can't measure this, so I think we sometimes skip this step before we sit down to write. I'd add that we also need to learn, learn, learn. Lenin is said to have urged the latter. . . .

At any rate, because I'm a Lacanian, I guess I've always been interested in the idea of recognition. It's important to his formulation of subjectivity, and he's in at least partial debt to Hegel. Here are some passages that include the term *recognition*, passages that I highlighted many, many years ago from those very books that I just mentioned. I apparently marked these particular passages to see if I might read them alongside Lacan, perhaps Hegel. Today, I find that I can't. I mean maybe, but it'd be a stretch. In the physical copies of my books, then, are evidence of my more youthful misreadings. Still, I suppose these passages represent some of the things that bounce around in my mind, some of the things that influence me, whether or not I'm fully conscious of them.

From *The Spivak Reader*:

> Our own arena of practice is the production of theoretical discourse. This practice would be significantly altered if it recognized that the theoretical discourse were irreducibly iterable (and it is a mark of the necessary "impurity" of a graphic that such recognition must come through the very conscious intention that the graphic calls into question).[2]

This passage is the one that's the most stretched. Really, Spivak is just talking about Derrida's notion of iterability here. I think she gets it more right than how Judith Butler seemed to understand it when she used it to develop her idea of performativity. For Derrida, the *–able* of *iterable* is important. It turns on a potentiality, whereas Butler's use of it only works if you have actual repetition, something that exhausts the potentiality. It's a subtle difference, but these are sometimes of great importance. However, the way Spivak uses recognition isn't in a technical way as my marginal notes would indicate.

From *Essentially Speaking*:

> No allowance is made for the historical production of these categories which would necessitate a recognition that what the classical Greeks understood by "man" and "woman" is radically different from what the Renaissance French understood them to signify or even what the contemporary postindustrial, postmodernist, poststructuralist theoretician is likely to understand by these terms.[3]

Again, recognition isn't so much of a technical term here as it is in Lacan. I probably highlighted this because I was trying to make a connection to how Lacan points out that "man" and "woman" are but signifiers, but because signifiers don't really signify – and I realize how counterintuitive this might seem – but only signs, this doesn't quite fit my purposes either. The ideas aren't as compatible as I maybe had been thinking.

From West's *Keeping Faith*:

> An inescapable aspect of this struggle was that the black diasporan peoples' quest for validation and recognition occurred on the ideological, social and cultural terrains of other nonblack peoples.[4]

I think here, I got excited about the word *ideological*. I thought I could read this alongside my most favorite Lacanian, Slavoj Žižek. But again, now that I know more, when I read this passage in context, it doesn't make the connection that I thought it might.

I continue to be interested in the concept of recognition. Here are some of the newer things that bounce around in my mind now. Let's wipe off the Cheetos dust from my Kindle, shall we?

Here's something I highlighted from Julietta Singh's *Unthinking Mastery*:

> In the anticolonial moment, mastery largely assumed a Hegelian form in which anticolonial actors were working through a desire or demand for recognition by another.[5]

Another thing from Stefano Harney and Fred Moten's *The Undercommons*:

> And I think a whole lot of what people want when they want reparations is in fact an acknowledgment, and they want an acknowledgement of the debt because it constitutes something like a form of recognition,

and that becomes very problematic because the form of recognition that they want is within an already existing system.[6]

And one more from Erica Burman's *Fanon, Education, Action*:

> There is also considerable overlap in analytic framework and political project between Freire and Fanon. Both address questions of (lack of) recognition as well as the role of formal education as a mode of subjugation alongside its emancipatory potential.[7]

These are the things I've been thinking with, particularly as I write this book. Although I won't spell how here so as to not spoil everything in advance, I plan to return to the underlying ideas in the chapters where I talk about Kojève and the Hegelian dialectic. The first two are, in fact, addressing Hegel, Singh explicitly, and Moten implicitly. Well, that's at least how I read him now. Maybe in another two and a half decades, I'll change my mind. And Burman's passage on Freire and Fanon makes me think of the university discourse. Fanon, of course, was a Lacanian himself. I'd say more about how passages serve to scaffold some of my own thought, but this would be to give away too many spoilers. I'm trying to work against the impatience that scholarly readers surprisingly have. It's an impatience that would perhaps have a mystery novel writer spell out in an introduction, "In this novel, I will show how the childhood friend of the protagonist is murdered by his own son-in-law. This will lead to a dramatic pursuit involving trains, and it will end with the protagonist being in a position to kill the son-in-law, though he chooses instead to spare his life."

Because this is not only a preface but also an acknowledgment section – although I know enough not to name it that, because I feel that these are too often skipped – I would also like to thank my good friend John Liberatore. After having instilled in me an appreciation of Jo Kondo, Josquin des Prez, and Buffalo Trace, he suggested that I read John Cage's *Silence: Lectures and Writings*. Reading that book started me on my current career trajectory. You should check out the former John's music. He has an album of compositions called *Line Drawings*. It was a nice companion to writing this book, and I imagine that it'll be a good companion when reading it. I particularly enjoy the composition "a tree-sprout, a nameless weed."

And, of course, thanks, Boo Boo.

Notes

1 For this book in particular, I'd also like to thank Matt Bickerton at Routledge and W. J. Dymond, my careful copyeditor.

2 Spivak, *The Spivak Reader*, 88.
3 Fuss, *Essentially Speaking*, 3.
4 West, *Keeping Faith*, 16.
5 Singh, *Unthinking Mastery*, 3.
6 Harney and Moten, *The Undercommons*, 152.
7 Burman, *Fanon, Education, Action*, 27.

1 Giving it away from the start

At the parting of the ways, paradise isn't lost

Let's not bury the lead. The guiding principle of the present work – a general principle for living flourishing lives together – is this:

> Nothing will be lost when everything is given away.

Thus, we ought to share fearlessly.

Now that I have the opportunity to engage in some projects of my own, I'm going to follow this insight strictly. Going beyond simply imagining utopian spaces, I here outline the architecture of how we can build and maintain things that don't reproduce old-boys networks or unfair hierarchies that benefit only an elite few who control an exploited many. These are the plans and principles for institutional structures that are minimally exclusive, structures that aim to be self-organizing. I believe that self-organizing structures are the only way to eventually avoid re-creating an unfairly ruling elite, one that will only have to be dismantled yet again. This isn't, however, a pitch for anarchy. Self-organizing structures are but a way to have maximally shared governance. Just as how the greatest ideological trick of capitalism is the club good – something that amounts to convincing everyone that they ought to pay for a non-rival resource – the greatest scam the old-boys network ever pulled was to convince us that they aren't completely unnecessary. In other words, those who keep their lofty positions of power all to themselves have somehow managed to get us to act as though we're unable to govern ourselves as a cooperating collective. There are other ways.

In what's to come, I'll outline plans for producing (1) dissertations without anxieties of influence, (2) conferences without directors, (3) journals without gatekeepers, (4) large-sample peer review, and (5) teaching beyond the university discourse.

And just to be absolutely clear, this book isn't an outline of how I will lead. Nor is this a book about how someone else should've led or should be leading. It isn't even a prescription for how to lead addressed to a person yet to come. It isn't any of these things because the answer to the question about who should lead us is this: the totality of anyone and *everyone* who's genuinely committed to doing good. And this excludes folks who are clever enough to know how to not look bigoted or oppressive by paying lip service in the language of resistance – those who secretly and reluctantly only do the minimum because they feel forced to "check a box," as they'd put it – but who are, in fact, hell-bent on upholding the status quo because it's to their own personal gain. You can't have just a few people taking up most of the space. Let's all leave room for each other because that room isn't as limited as some might have you believe.

This is a book about how we all can share responsibly by sharing responsibilities. I acknowledge that much of the building and maintenance we'll be doing will consist of unrecognized work. So be it. At the end of the day, that cost is worth it, for sharing fairly is immeasurably better than this cycle we've been unable to break. Still, we need as many people as we can get on board. This is why I feel that no plans regarding what we must build should be secret, no knowledge proprietary. Sharing the blueprints is necessary, for it's only through sharing and transparency that we, as a community, can grow and develop the good that should've belonged to each and every one of us from the start.

* * *

The primary insight of this book comes from John Cage. It can be found in *Silence: Lectures and Writings*:

> But this fearlessness only follows if, at the parting of the ways, where it is realized that sounds occur whether intended or not, one turns in the direction of those he does not intend. This turning is psychological and seems at first to be a giving up of everything that belongs to humanity – for a musician, the giving up of music. This psychological turning leads to the world of nature, where, gradually or suddenly, one sees that humanity and nature, not separate, are in this world together; that nothing was lost when everything was given away.[1]

Apart from its epic knowledge drop at the end, I like this passage not only because it's nicely posthuman in the way that it doesn't cordon off humanity from nature but also because it challenges what it means to be a composer. Why are we so certain that the minimum criteria of being a composer – perhaps a musician in general – is that one's output consists only of what's completely within one's own control? What if we were to give up on this notion? What would music be like? And moving from composer and musician to editor and writer, what might this mean?

In some sense, to make an analogy here doesn't quite fit. If the musician simply follows the composer, then the musician submits to the will of the composer, and it's the composer whose will is fully realized. However, one might argue that if one is a writer, then one is less a musician but more of a composer themselves, for clearly we think of a composer – at least in the traditional sense that Cage questions – as being a sort of writer. I feel, however, that this latter argument can only be comfortably made given that one has never been the recipient of a rejection letter.

Regarding publishing, because of the way things have been set up, the writer can't help but feel that they're not completely in control. A writer may write what they please, but in order to become a published author – in order to be recognized for one's work – what one has written must conform to an editor's own will. If this is so, then at best, when staring down a blank page, one writes not only for oneself but also for what one imagines to be the will of an editor. At worst, say if publication were an absolute necessity, one may find oneself writing only for what one imagines to be an editor's will. Then, upon receiving a revise and resubmit, one writes for what no longer must be imagined. And by this extension, one can also write for the will of imagined or actual peer reviewers. And by that extension, one may find oneself writing for the will of folks who might eventually review one's tenure or promotion portfolio, for one's non-reviewer peers, even for online trolls given that altmetrics are now a thing. The way things have been set up, the writer who'd be recognized as author must potentially submit to several wills.

Is there a way out of this? I think maybe there is. Either we completely give up on the notion of publishing being of the highest value – and for the academic, this would involve major changes to the institution of the university – or folks finding themselves in the position of regulating the flow of information change the rules such that even the academy's slow to change institutional practices might hurry up a bit. Publishing is indeed a valuable product. It's necessary. However, this isn't to say that we've gotten everything right about it, nor is it to say that it's the only valuable thing. There are several valuable processes and products in which we partake, all along in our paths through academe, especially in our capacity as content producers.

Gatekeeper, doorperson, collector

For anyone acting in a capacity of deciding on what scholarship gets disseminated – publisher, editor, reviewer, yes, but also anyone regulating any particular medium for scholarly content producers – let's start from a simple premise. Gatekeeping: bad.

It's better that anyone responsible for regulating the flow of scholarly information see themselves as more of a doorperson. What does a doorperson do? A doorperson opens the door for people who have business inside, only refusing access when (1) one clearly has no business and (2) the inside is filled to capacity. Thus, a good principle for deciding about scholarly dissemination is to first ask oneself: Could this piece of scholarship have any business being disseminated to the scholarly community? In other words, regardless of whether I agree with what's contained in this scholarly piece of work, is it the case that to the best of my own judgment, the scholarly content potentially has something good to contribute? If the answer is yes, then one should make a reasonable effort to disseminate it. Doorpersoning: good.

Still, there are a few things yet to consider. If one is a doorperson editor who edits a publication with a limited page budget, one finds oneself having to reject otherwise good manuscripts because there's no room inside. Furthermore, one editor and maybe a few reviewers are perhaps too small a sample size to determine whether an article has value. Sure, one could paraphrase Churchill here and say that all this may be the worst possible of all systems but the best one we have, but I'm not sure that's exactly true given the possibilities offered by digital media.

What if we retooled the process of scholarly production? Why shouldn't it be the case, for instance, that we use digital repositories like ResearchGate not for post-publication peer review but for peer review itself? In other words, why not post manuscripts in a digital repository first? This way, scholarship is available to the community as soon as it's deemed ready by the author. This has the virtue of timeliness, something preferable to good work sitting around in a journal's backlog that may be two to three years if it's without online prepublication. The good articles get recommendations from readers. Thus, peer review isn't limited to just a few people but is expanded to a large scholarly community online. If we do this, then what would be the task of the editor? The editor would scour the repository for articles that they may like to publish, using the number of recommendations and comments as a guide. The editor's task is to become an expert curator. Furthermore, what if an editor had unlimited space to collect? If the digital repository is unlimited, why should any subset of that repository be limited if also digital? Collecting: maybe the best. This might be true for traditionally structured journals, but it can be even more true for a differently structured type of journal, a journal without an editor but which is assembled by a crowdsourced set of vetted reviews. The journal itself becomes the collection not of a single collector, but more on this later.

Sleep furiously, colorless green ideas

Here's a riddle from "A Crazy Mixed-Up Day: Thirty Brainteasers," a text Walter Benjamin prepared for a youth-hour radio broadcast. It's couched in a story about a person named Heinz. Heinz has awoken sleepily, for he had been troubled by a riddle during the night. He then goes to find his friend Anton, an "absent-minded professor type," who enjoys riddle solving.[2]

> If each day a bookworm eats through one volume in a series of books, how long will it take for it to eat its way from the first page of one volume to the last page of the next, provided he eats in the same direction in which the series of books is arranged?[3]

Before I call absent-minded professor types nerdy bookworms, let me preface that I've always identified as both myself. At least my mom had identified me as the latter almost every time I went out to play. "Why do you dress like an old man?" she'd say. "Don't the other kids make fun of you?" Granted, I didn't go out to play very much. I spent a lot of time trying to read through all the volumes of our encyclopedia. I started this project over several times, each time in earnest to yet an even higher degree. I know a bunch of stuff about aardvarks.

Many of us bookworms grow up to become absent-minded professors. I'm not certain that it isn't our bookishness that's responsible for several of our methodological practices. For instance, why was it that most of my peers sported mullets or teased bangs and combined acid-washed denim with neon-colored T-shirts? They looked out into the world and saw that that's what everyone in their peer group seemed to be doing; then they put that knowledge to work. For them, this came naturally. As for myself, I only notice those things now when looking at old high school photos. Like I do today, I apparently wore oxford button-downs and gray or navy chinos.

Back in the day, I didn't really notice what's now overwhelmingly noticeable. I was too single-mindedly busy trying to learn how to play jazz. By that time, I had given up on my dictionary project, and I had read all but one volume of our encyclopedia. We bought single volumes at a discounted price from the grocery store each week, but one week, we didn't go. But again, my point is that in my single-minded focus on my extremely narrow interest, I missed a bunch of everything else.

Noticing what everyone was doing – which seemed to come easy for almost everyone else – took a lot of effort on my part. I had to go about it in a way that approximated scientific rigor: "What is it, exactly, that makes gray chinos nerdy? Is it the material, the color, the looser cut, all, or a combination of these? In my granddad's time, they weren't nerdy at all, and all the cool jazz folks wore them, too. But it appears that values have changed. What brought this about? Is it a single thing, or is it rather a constellation of things coming together in this historical present? Furthermore, is this change in values geographically confined? Perhaps I should go to the mall and carefully observe the cool kids. I shall have to take field notes." Anyway, having inserted some sufficient suspense, here's the answer to Benjamin's riddle:

> The bookworm needs only a moment to get from the first page of the first book to the last page of the second, because in a properly arranged library, the first page of the first book is right up against the last page of the second.[4]

This might also be the answer to a riddle we have ourselves, although not necessarily one that we've been trying to solve. The bookworm performs what seems to be a time-warp jump but only if you figure that it's eating from left to right from the perspective of the front-facing edges of a bookshelf. It could be eating from left to right from the perspective of the back-facing edges. Similarly, my fashion sensibilities had been both behind and ahead of their time inasmuch as they continue, if I do say so myself, to be timeless.

We professor types – both absent- and present-minded alike – who self-fashion as visionaries often awake sleepless, having been troubled by the riddle of "What comes next?" And being professor types, we seek out the help of our friends, much like Heinz, by looking to their cutting-edge scholarship. The trouble is, is that the cutting-edge scholarship we look to generally consists of published books and articles. However, published books and articles take some time to write and even more time to bring to publication. What seems to have just come out the other day is already at least a few years old by the time we get to read it. So we base our articles about the future of the discipline on things that are already not new, and by the time folks get to read our predictions about the future, that prediction itself is a few years old. But maybe our problem isn't that we make mistakes on our path to finding answers but that we start with the wrong riddle. Like the bookworm, we don't need to be eating through books in any particular direction. Thus, we might turn around and not be so obsessed with what comes next but rather look to what's come before.

Tradition is important, and it could be our future. This is so long as we don't treat tradition as a sacred ritual, guard it jealously as though any one of us could own it, and thus have the absolute authority to dictate what it must or mustn't be or take ourselves so seriously while partaking in it that one can't even enjoy a self-deprecating joke about one's own field of study.

Furthermore, it isn't lost on me that many of the suggestions that I'll be making regarding how we might do things differently aren't new but are things people have been doing for a long time now, only in contexts other than academe. Maybe we feel that the way we do things has the virtue of being timeless, but maybe in our single-minded focus on our narrow interests, we've let good things pass us by. Not all haircuts and denim treatments are ridiculous years later. Some things that were once new eventually become time-tested practices. In these cases, better retro than never.

Throwback

In the digital age, this really isn't something that's practiced, but in the days when people submitted actual handwritten writing – whether in one's own script or typed on a mechanical typewriter – rejected manuscripts were physically returned. This practice of returning rejected manuscripts lies more closely to the literal meaning of rejection itself: to throw back. And whereas I probably wouldn't have wanted my handwritten manuscript thrown back at me, there's something nice in the gesture of this return. When a manuscript is handwritten, the effort of the writing is recognizable in the physical manifestation of the writing itself. Some editor or reviewer or committee chair may not have liked the content, but that one cares enough to return it at least acknowledges that a manuscript has some kind of intrinsic value, if only that of someone having painstakingly put letters on many, many a page. So even if they didn't like it, I can't imagine, for instance, that anyone would've literally thrown out the first version of what was to become Walter Benjamin's *The Origin of German Tragic Drama*. In fact, although it may not have been thrown out, it was indeed rejected.

Think about that for a moment. I sometimes like to contemplate it myself: Walter Benjamin's *The Origin of German Tragic Drama* was originally rejected. In other words, after having had a look through what would eventually become one of the foundational texts for modern literary criticism, through clenched teeth and a grimace, someone probably made an audible backward sigh and, after what was perhaps but a brief pause, thought: nope. Actually, we know through Benjamin's letters to Gershom Scholem that such a someone was one Professor Schultz, the equivalent of the department chair of where Benjamin was trying to submit the manuscript as his doctoral thesis. I sometimes like to tell friends who've just received a rejection letter, one unaccompanied by a physically returned manuscript, what I sometimes like to contemplate. "In the digital age," I begin, "this really isn't something that's practiced, but . . ."

So rejections didn't used to be acts of a literal throwing out. They can't literally be that today either; digital copies are both only digital and only copies. Still, in whatever era one finds oneself, I'm sure that having a manuscript rejected feels like having one's work literally thrown out. And if contemplating Benjamin's originally rejected manuscript doesn't help, perhaps contemplating a passage from the final version will. The passage is from the prologue, one that Benjamin calls "Epistemo-Critical." Excluding an epigraph from Goethe, they're the very first words to the only completed book Benjamin ever properly published:

> It is characteristic of philosophical writing that it must continually confront the question of representation. In its finished form philosophy will, it is true, assume the quality of doctrine, but it does not lie within the power of mere thought to confer such a form. Philosophical doctrine is based on historical codification. It cannot therefore be evoked *more geometrico*. The more clearly mathematics demonstrate that the total elimination of the problem of representation – which is boasted by every proper didactic system – is the sign of genuine knowledge, the more conclusively does it reveal its renunciation of that area of truth towards which language is directed.[5]

If, on some level, to philosophize is to think in a certain way, then Benjamin is suggesting that thinking alone doesn't give philosophy the quality of a doctrine. In other words, think all the thoughts that you want – represent things to yourself – but philosophizing doesn't achieve the gravitas of being doctrinal until it's recognized as significant through the representation that is a historical codification. And how might we interpret what's meant by historical codification? Were we attempting to discern a doctrine from Benjamin's own work, perhaps we'd read it in the light of his "Theses on the Philosophy of History," but given the context of the reception of *The Origin of German Tragic Drama* itself, perhaps there's another possible set of interpretations: Apart from an actual historical archive of actual manuscripts – one like the one that now exists for Benjamin – and given that codification can't happen without the possibility of the written, to historically codify, one might say, could consist of having something published. Put simply, if you don't publish it, all that intellectual labor doesn't seem to count. I think these are a nice first few sentences given the text's own prior history of having been denied doctrine bestowing representation. Here, it isn't so much that Benjamin is showing up actual or would-be detractors of his work but giving us a subversive acknowledgment of how things are. Acknowledgments of the way things are, of course, aren't always tacit approvals of the status quo. Rather, they're often the necessary first steps toward critique. And here, what's being acknowledged is how intellectual work itself often goes unacknowledged. For every published text that becomes part of philosophical history, what vast amounts of unpublished intellectual work are we necessarily unaware of? And what if somewhere within these vast amounts of unpublished intellectual work are important disclosures of truth?

And what about the last half of the passage in question? Doesn't this sound like the complaint of a qualitative researcher? Our thinking isn't reducible to statistics, formulas, or data that we've computed somehow. In our own epistemo-critical moments, don't we ourselves wish to challenge the notion that numbers alone are the "the sign of genuine knowledge"? Don't we wish to point out how when a more positivistic research practice claims this, that "the more conclusively does it reveal its renunciation of that area of truth towards which language is directed"? Oriented as such, positivistic approaches to social science wouldn't merely reject our work, they'd reject a whole procedure of disclosing truth.

While I don't deny that mathematics can indeed explain many things, not all truth is discovered through math alone. To think in such a way is to be sutured to one truth procedure when the procedures are multiple. At bottom, if we're qualitative researchers, we don't merely dabble in trying to answer the question of representation. We continually confront it as would any philosopher. And sometimes, like Benjamin, we get our manuscripts rejected. This isn't, however, to say that we aren't doing good work.

Hey, teacher!

This is from a lecture collected in Jacques Lacan's *Talking to Brick Walls*:

> I can easily forgive this person for putting my name – which is explained by the fact that she was standing in front of me – in the place of what would have been more appropriate, namely *my discourse*. You see, I'm not ducking out. I call it mine. We shall be seeing in a while whether this *my* deserves to be maintained. . . . I will stress right away that this speech is speech designed for teaching. On this occasion, I set teaching apart from discourse.[6]

Not all of one's discourses are one's teaching. There are other discourses that might be ours serving other purposes. Furthermore, not all of our writing is meant for publication. That's something that's easily forgotten given the pressure we might feel to publish, a pressure much stronger than the one exerted on us to teach. Odd, in light of the fact that it's perhaps our teaching that's of greatest importance.

Publish or perish is as they say, but we need to rethink a system that can punish us for continuing to do good work that doesn't result in publication, for on the other side of this, were publication to be the only motivation for doing the work we do, many things of importance wouldn't get done. For instance, (1) we'd never bother writing dissertations, (2) we'd never partake in conferences for their own sake, (3) we'd never make scholarly connections through social or online media, (4) we'd never do any reviews, and (5) perhaps what's worst of all, no teaching would ever happen. Without any one of these things, we don't even have an academic community to begin with. And when we do seek to publish, to not be fully caught up in this system that needs to be rethought, we should be able to answer yes to the following question: *Would I continue to do the work that I do were the condition of publication to entail the effacement of my signature?*

As scholars, we do a lot of things that can be considered writing, broadly defined. Writing, in a sense, is any kind of recorded communication. Much of this writing constitutes unrecognized work. Regarding this unrecognized work, not only can unrecognized work have turned out to have been the product of a choice-worthy pursuit, but it's also often choice-worthy to pursue the good in ways wherein it's all but a foregone conclusion that our work will never be recognized. We're led to believe that it's all about the publications. However, when it comes down to it, our work output doesn't consist only of publication, nor is it the case that we've done no good work if we've not been able to publish. Although it may go unacknowledged, let's please not stop doing the good work that we do.

The first type of good yet unrecognized work that we do consists of writing dissertations.

Notes

1 Cage, *Silence: Lectures and Writings*, 8.
2 Benjamin, "A Crazy Mixed-Up Day: Thirty Brainteasers," 190.
3 Ibid., 195.
4 Ibid., 196.
5 Benjamin, *The Origin of German Tragic Drama*, 27.
6 Lacan, *Talking to Brick Walls*, 38–39.

2 Dissertations

Rey of lightsaber (intro)

This is from Bill Germano himself. It's from his book *From Dissertation to Book*:

> To judge by the manuscripts that scholars send to publishing houses, the majority of the theses for which the PhD is awarded are still highly limited enterprises – confident treatments of narrow subjects, making claims to boldness but doing so by means of elaborate reference to the work of others . . . your dissertation may be looking backward to be sure it's safe from Foucault, Freud, Butler, Bhabha, Agamben, and other widely cited thinkers – not that any of them are threatening you or your thesis in any way. To disarm your deities, you cite, paraphrase, and incorporate the ideas of leading scholars now at work. You pour libations to the loudest of the influential dead. The more you do this, the more difficult it becomes to see where your own work ends and the ideas of the masters begin, so thoroughly has your writing absorbed a way of expressing itself.[1]

If you're reading this and you've just started out on your path as a scholar, you might be in the midst of writing what's probably the longest document you've ever written, one that maybe four people will read. For short, we've traditionally called such an undertaking a dissertation. When writing your dissertation, I'd say that one of the most important things is to situate your work in the relevant traditions. You don't need to start from scratch, and you shouldn't. It's best to innovate from the state of the art, and to fully understand the state of the art, you need to understand how we got there. Still, I agree with Germano. We do pour libations to the loudest of the influential dead. And I guess, by that token, if we don't idolize the loudest of the living, maybe we have imaginary symposia with them? This doesn't seem to stop with the dissertation, though. More than the anxiety of influence – which is, incidentally, the title of a book by Harold Bloom – our point should be to not get stuck here. Without needing to forget or destroy it, we do need to think beyond what has come before, if for anything, because contexts change. It's like what Emerson says in a commencement speech he made, "The American Scholar." Apart from its epic failure to recognize contributions of anyone other than men, I think it speaks a truth:

> Meek young men grow up in libraries, believing it their duty to accept the views, which Cicero, which Locke, which Bacon, have given, forgetful that Cicero, Locke, and Bacon were only young men in libraries, when they wrote these books.[2]

And was I just now stringing together references ironically? Sadly, I can only play it off in retrospect.

Still, even more importantly with respect to positioning oneself in relation to what's come before, I think it's good to remember that writing from tradition doesn't mean that you get caught up in quarrels that were never yours to begin with. Definitely don't feel like you need to inherit those. Anyway, there are several of these quarrels. Some big ones are (1) quantitative versus qualitative, (2) the social sciences versus the sciences, or (3) the humanities versus people into posthumanism. And within any discipline, there are quarrels within those, too, not to mention theoretical or methodological quarrels within subdisciplines, not to mention graduate faculty in your program, and not to mention people's own internal conflicts. It's like a quarrel fractal. Avoid. I myself did through the good fortune of having some really, really wonderful committee members. Life was good.

Furthermore, granted that folks on your dissertation committee might find themselves spiraling through this fractal, don't let them turn you into their foot soldiers and weaponize your talent. For one thing, for all the militant talk that you might hear in reference to academic work, this is obviously never anything like a war. Personally, I think using war as a metaphor for anything is troublesome in light of those who've actually experienced or are experiencing war. In any case, in general, we probably shouldn't be thinking about disagreements as any kind of fight at all. A wise friend often tells me that reasonable people can disagree. Still, that won't stop certain types of folks who could be on your committee from trying to pull you into the messes that they've made with others. They'll recognize your talent and try to use it against colleagues of theirs who, for some reason or another, they find threatening. Maybe your committee member is a big name in your field. Maybe you want a high-profile recommendation letter. You might've been promised a co-authored book chapter, paper, or some other shiny thing, but all these could be a deal with the devil. When it feels like it is, don't meet at the crossroads, because at the end of the day, you won't even be able to play any better than you would've with patient practice. Besides, don't you probably like jazz guitar better than acoustic blues? Furthermore, if you're talented enough, you'll also be threatening to any such folks in the vortex. It'll seem like they're pulling you through, but their offerings are just ways to keep you under their thumb. Also avoid. There's no need to petrify any of this in Dissertation Abstracts International.

Don't avoid thinking and writing for yourself. Trust your ability to develop your own skills. That's how you got into your graduate program to begin with. Yes, you do need to be networked, because no one can do any of this alone, but find your own family, one composed of people who, in reversing the fractal, have the best interests of you, your field, and the world in mind. True, even if you discover that you're Emperor Palpatine's granddaughter, that's not the life you need to choose. Your found family will help you because they know what kind of contribution you'll make. They may be difficult to come by, but trust me, your family is out there. Come find us.

Look, use the forks (lit review)

They always give you way too tiny plastic plates at departmental cocktail parties. I've found a way around this by fastening three of them together to make one regular-sized plate. More *crudités* for me! Yay?

Jasmine and I – hi, Boo Boo – are fond of telling our students that academic writing is like joining an already-ongoing conversation at one of these parties. It's a common metaphor, useful to some extent. Still, I'm not sure what cocktail party conversations include statements such as "I'm sorry to interrupt, but I heard you speaking about the wine. Although you're somewhat correct that 'It's good,' as you say, you fail to notice the clash of secondary and tertiary aromas, something to which only a sommelier, or someone with a refined palate such as myself, can speak." Still, we can find such remarks in the deficit discourses of literature reviews: "While surname and surname (year) are correct about this or that, their study fails to do this awesome thing that I'm about to do!" [mic drop].

For real, though, could we just not? First, no need to tell people that their whole thing is wrong. But for the wrong stuff, just maybe don't cite it. Second, no need to self-aggrandize. How did any of this become a standard writing practice? To put this into Hegelian terms – and, as a Marxist, why wouldn't I? – the source of the problem might be failing to think beyond the first part of the dialectic of the lord and bondsman.

High Marx (methods)

It was circa 1994. I was a biology major. Why was a biology major hanging out in the Marxist section of the hippie campus bookstore that smelled of book smell and pot? The then love of my life, whom I had been too scared to really ever talk to, was a Marxist. I knew her from high school. She was fearlessly incendiary. She wasn't afraid to call out all the nuns on their nun sense, never tucked in her oxford blouse, nor would she even stand for the Pledge. The sticker on her English class folder read "Capitalism = Racism." I didn't quite get it, so she explained. After that, I got it, kind of. When I kind of got to college, I had a vague fantasy that I'd graduate, go to med school, end up working with or for her parents in some hospital or clinic, and at long last – wandering around at a cocktail party, maybe – be reunited. Sure, that might not be for another decade, but by then, I should probably know at least something about Marxism. In ten years, I could probably be an expert, and that, I figured, could be the way to finally start up a conversation. For some reason, in this fantasy, I'd also be looking in the distance, sipping a glass of wine, something which I also had ten years to learn about.

Although I may not have learned much about what the hippocampus does – and it's totally not contradictory for a Marxist to be really into wine – I did learn a bunch about alienated labor, hegemony, and ideological interpellation. I suppose I can't not admit that that fantasy lasted at least long enough to get that far. Also, I wasn't sure which Marxism, so I read a lot of it. Also, I probably should've realized that her Marxist parents weren't even that kind of doctor.

At a certain age, resistance, in general, is appealing. Marcuse's *One-Dimensional Man*, for instance, had been mind-blowing, for it so brilliantly articulated everything that I thought I had already brilliantly discovered in the brilliant manuscript which was my as-of-yet bedside notebook. Such books, however, share the same fate of *Catcher in the Rye*. Later on in life, we can let those books get dusty or use them to level a crooked bed. Alexandre Kojève's lectures collected in *Introduction to the Reading of Hegel*, however, really stuck with me. Not only does that book put into context and make sense of most, if not, to some extent, all, poststructuralist philosophy – it's sort of the big secret book of big secrets when it comes to that – but it also describes how we tend to behave badly as academics. One can't read it and not find the fight to the death for recognition as all too familiar. One wonders if Hegel wasn't talking about his colleagues, and if he was, Kojève must've identified.

We humans desire to be recognized. This would otherwise entail a fight to the death with other humans, but if you end up actually killing those you overcome, then there's no one left to recognize you. Thus, if you want to be the master, you instead dominate them, and once you do, you retain their recognition. However, you find this is no good because when you compare yourself to all who recognize you, you find that they aren't up to your level. But in an unforeseen twist, this surprisingly leaves the dominated in the better position. Although dominated, they realize that competing for the prestige of recognition is BS and choose instead to *not* partake in this fight to the death. Knowing that this set up doesn't quite work, the dominated are "ready for change; in [their] very being, [they are] change, transcendence, transformation, 'education.'"[3] Furthermore, according to this narrative, it will be the dominated who will come to transform the world through their work.

It's all about Walter Benjamin's (findings)

Here's an interesting find I made while researching Benjamin's dissertation. It's from *Walter Benjamin: The Production of an Intellectual Figure* by Sandra Vivian Berta Hoenle, which itself is an unpublished dissertation:

> In his analysis of Benjamin's relationship to the university, Irving Wohlfarth convincingly characterizes Schultz as a "political animal who knew how to change his tack, blow hot and cold, keep a low profile, stay out of trouble, pass the buck, play by the rules, etc." ("Resentment Begins at Home" 230). According to Wohlfarth, Schultz's "calculated duplicity toward an exceptional candidate who might, if admitted to the profession, refuse to play the game" is a "tactical response to two contradictory pressures – the old-boy network which administers the status quo and the candidate's appeal to the standards by which the academic institution legitimizes itself" ("Resentment Begins at Home" 231). Wohlfarth has identified what Schultz was in his position . . . a master of the political game who attempted to maximize his own position while preserving the status quo. Schultz's behaviour and actions exemplify the usually unarticulated and generally unexamined subtext underlying the production of knowledge within the institution of the university.[4]

That this is from a dissertation is interesting. I wonder if there's a hidden message here . . . like finding a Kinder Surprise Egg during Easter.

No, that isn't what the constant comparative method is (discussion)

This is from Lacan's *Seminar III*:

> In true speech the Other is that before which you make yourself recognized. But you can make yourself recognized by it only because it

is recognized first. It has to be recognized for you to be able to make yourself recognized.[5]

The Other for Lacan is the treasury of signifiers. For our purposes regarding the system of the university, we can think of this Other as being something like the library of all things published, the thing to which, as scholars, we're supposed to contribute. We write in the discourse of the university, and perhaps, we speak in the dialect of a particular scholarly tradition. That's how we come to be recognized as a scholar. The question of our scholarly identity is often asked in the form of "What's your research?" When we answer, we often indicate that our surname is the same as a methodological or philosophical tradition. It's expected that we bring honor to our family name.

If I've come to know anything about the academy, it's that the name of almost any scholarly tradition is a label for what we've come to agree on but only just as much as it's a label for the things we disagree about. There's no need for lasting consensus about what should be included in a scholarly tradition. A lack of consensus doesn't mean that we get stuck in the first part of Hegel's lord-and-bondsman dialectic either. In fact, consensus really ought not be our goal. Reasonable people can disagree, and sometimes, they should. Innovation and adaptation can't happen without the possibility of disagreement, and we should understand that scholarly traditions aren't the same thing as rituals.

That being said, let me repeat that I still don't think it's a good idea to start on one's path by competing against others for prestige. There's never a need to. Recognition isn't a limited resource, so there's no need to maintain a system that makes it artificially so. Knowledge produced through scholarly traditions can be a public good, especially now that we do have technologies to make knowledge available in ways that can be widely accessible. However, some people do spend a lot of energy actively working to limit access to make knowledge a club good. It isn't easy to make an accessible, non-rival resource such that nonpaying people can't enjoy it, but capitalism, we should note, always finds clever ways to disprove the existence of public goods in its never-ending search for finding techniques of exclusion. For instance, regarding the light from a lighthouse, is it difficult to imagine that someday, capitalism will retroactively make incorrect even this standard example? Why not, say, use infrared light and charge for the goggles? Exclusion is always a win–win situation, only one wherein the capitalist wins twice: in our example, making money at the harbor and creating a compelling reason to sell revised editions of expensive economics textbooks.

The fact of the matter is that exclusion is immensely profitable, and because capitalism has no requirement of being ethical, capitalism also produces an immense amount of unfairness as a by-product. If we partake in such a system when we have a choice not to, then we're complicit with this unfairness. And if we're scholars who claim to be critically minded, we should really do better not to leave the ideology of artificially limiting recognition as unquestioned.

For instance, although I understand that the intentions behind things such as awards for the best research of this or that sort are well-intentioned – I helped create some, in fact – let's examine the logic of all this. Is it good that hard work is recognized? Yes, of course it is. So in a large conference of several thousand, we have awards that recognize the best paper in a division or special interest group of several hundred. We give awards for outstanding this or outstanding that. Some journals even give out awards for their best articles. Well-deserved recognition? Sure. However, focusing on recognizing only the very top – and maybe an honorable mention or two – means that you recognize everything else as being of lesser value somehow. It's almost as if to say, "Don't waste your time with any of that other stuff." But is attention and time so limited that we can we really say that only the best three of hundreds are worthy of recognition? No, we can't say that either. And in the first place, what does it mean to be in the top three? To determine a ranking, one has to have criteria, but I can't think of any criteria that seem nonarbitrary. The most well written? Who's to say, really? The most innovative? How can one determine that? The most cited? Well, there's the fact that citation metrics don't specify whether people are citing you because they like your work or if, instead, they're using it as an example of a mistake that shouldn't be made. But more important, why should most popular qualify as best? At the end of the day, the ideology of *best* and *most* artificially minimizes the number of things that can be of value.

Furthermore, many of us have bought into the idea of being a top scholar. But what does such a thing even mean? Whatever it means, the pursuit of it starts, kind of, when one gets to college. You had been told that you should get into the best undergraduate program, which if you're so inclined, is more or less necessary to get into the best graduate program. You want to get into the best graduate program so that when you graduate, you can be hired at one of the best universities. There, you can compete more to get tenured, and if you continue to compete and become a top scholar in your field, you eventually get promoted to full. True, if you're in a technological field, being at one of the top universities has its use. Top universities have the resources to get the equipment one needs for research, and this can be expensive. If you aren't in a technological field needing expensive equipment, being at a top university means you have on-campus access to the most comprehensive libraries. That used to mean something before interlibrary loans and the Internet. And if publicly funded research weren't behind a paywall at all – there's some movement in this direction in the US – library access would even be less of an issue. Still, those of us who don't have to nonetheless compete.

Let's question, for a moment, why research positions are valued over teaching positions, why a teaching position is framed as something you may end up in if you don't follow the moral of some cautionary tale that someone on your dissertation committee might tell you. If community is as important as we educators say it is, why is teaching at a satellite or community college seen as only a lowly contribution? Teaching positions are choice-worthy pursuits, but they aren't often presented that way. If the dissemination of knowledge is the goal, this makes little sense. For instance, I was at a large midwestern university that boasted one of the largest university libraries. We had one copy of what I considered to be an important book in my field. It had been charged a total of three times since its publication: once in 1964, once in the 1970s, and then me. If that book did only as well at 499 other libraries, then I had much more of an audience in the decade I spent teaching.

Now, I'm not saying that there's no difference in capability between people. I'll again use myself as an example here: I know that I'm not as capable as some people, and I'm more capable than others. This is true for everyone with the exception of two people. It wouldn't be true for either the most capable person or the least. What I am saying, however, is that although you can spend your time ranking folks, the only reason to expend such energy is when you're considering how to best distribute limited resources. This isn't to make a value judgment on the worth of any particular individual but to make practical decisions about need or efficacy. If, let's say, it's the case that there's a limited resource that can be put to the good use of benefiting all, then we ought to put the most suited people in the position of using those resources for the good. For instance, if there are only a finite number of labs that can work on curing a disease, then for sure, don't even give me a job as a lab assistant. I haven't the necessary skills, nor can I attain them because I'm dispositionally unable. That aside, there's no reason to rank folks when the resource in question is limitless. This only leads to hurt feelings, at best, and unfair discrimination, at worst.

What I'm saying is that in terms of recognition, there's not really a need to distinguish between a top scholar and every other scholar. Recognition doesn't run out. Any of us who do our job of producing knowledge to be passed on through education is worthy of recognition. Furthermore, this recognition doesn't need to admit of degrees, because apart from lab access, I don't know what limited resource we'd be competing for. Our obsession with ordering ourselves from greatest to least isn't unlike a bad addiction. When there isn't any obvious benefit, but instead an obvious detriment, why do we feel so compelled to compare ourselves to our peers? It's enough to know that we're doing our own personal best. Why should it give us joy to know that we're achieving more than someone else, pain us to know we're doing worse? Let's maybe stop all that. There are better ways to expend our energy.

Still, I understand that not everyone will agree to this. Once you've found your family, however, as best we can, we'll collectively try to deal with these folks who make things unnecessarily difficult by still trying to dominate. Notwithstanding, that shouldn't stop any of us from continuing onward, onward as we attempt to transform the world through our work. But where might we gather?

Notes

1 Germano, *From Dissertation to Book*, 14.
2 Emerson, "The American Scholar," n.p.
3 Kojève, *Introduction to the Reading of Hegel*, 22.
4 Hoenle, *Walter Benjamin: The Production of an Intellectual Figure*, 123–124.
5 Lacan, *Book III*, 51.

3 Conferences

The Sixteenth International Congress

If you know only one of Jacques Lacan's writings, then you probably know "The Mirror Stage as Formative of the *I* Function as Revealed in Psychoanalytic Experience." There's a whole lot of scholarship based around it, especially in media and film studies, not to mention all the stuff that folks in literary studies did with it. And if you know that piece, you may rank it as a good contender for the densest six pages of text that you've ever tried to slog through. Although the piece is included in the *Écrits*, it's actually a conference paper. It was delivered at the Sixteenth International Congress of Psychoanalysis. Had that conference not happened, let's say, and that paper not been delivered, we might not really have cinema studies as we know it. That discipline really comes into its own with Laura Mulvey and Christian Metz, and Lacan's mirror stage essay was really important for both of them.

Recently, the Sixteenth International Congress of Qualitative Inquiry was canceled. I have to admit that part of my mind wandered to the thought, "What if there were a paper in the preliminary program that would've been delivered that would go on to shape several disciplines, and in fact more or less create one?" Regarding our little corner of the world, our qualitative corner, you might say, maybe that happened. The world may never know. That particular congress only exists as a frozen potentiality, one in the form of a .pdf that I have yet to upload to the website.

To quote or not to quote?

Jasmine and I attended the Modern Language Association conference in Chicago in 2019. We had visited my mom who lives really near Chicago, just outside of Gary, Indiana, and were in town, so we figured, why not? We got to see Judith Butler talk at one of the panels. She said something really interesting regarding oppressive regimes, something I haven't encountered in her writing since or after. It seemed to be more of an off-the-cuff remark in response to what was being discussed in the room, but it was no less brilliant for being extemporaneous. I wrote it down in my little book of philosophical field notes – thanks, Sarah Bridges-Rhoads – so I could at least make a paraphrase of it here, but I won't. There's something to be said for keeping certain things within smaller networks. You don't want the opposition to know your best strategies, necessarily. However, I do believe that knowledge should be shared. A possible compromise? If you find me and ask me about this quote from Judith Butler, I'll tell you. If Jasmine's around, she might give you a purple flower. And we don't necessarily have to meet in person to make such exchanges, especially since the purple flowers aren't really flowers, nor are they purple.

The dialectic of large and small networks

To some extent, conferences aren't simply networking opportunities, but the networks themselves. Several disciplines have mega-conference networks, and when any network gets big enough, it encounters the problems of any large organization: bureaucracy-encrusted hypocrisy. For instance, several conferences wherein scholars oriented toward justice make their disciplinary homes end up supporting things that their delegates don't. There are large conferences that take up the theme of environmental justice while themselves raising carbon emissions through necessitating travel that relies upon fossil fuels. Furthermore, such conferences may end up crossing picket lines when hotel staff are on strike. Other times, while claiming to be inclusive and calling for activism and resistance, they do nothing to fight bigotry within their very own organization. When problems such as these go beyond infrequent, isolated incidents and instead become rampant, our first reaction often tends to make moves toward dismantling the network supporting what we find to be hypocritical. And this is a good reaction. These sorts of networks need to go. However, the question becomes, What replaces a large network that's gone bad?

Typically, you do need to replace the badly acting large networks. You can't simply swap out the leadership, for the network creates its own particular subject positions of leadership, and anyone who comes to occupy one of those positions is left little choice but to become a bad actor. If you can't simply swap out the leadership, then you can't replace a large network with an equally large network. You can't simply move everyone from one network to another without reproducing the original network's architecture. If you reproduce the architecture, you must reproduce the subject positions of leadership, and that's what we don't want. Thus, you need to build a different architecture. When you build a different architecture, you need time to regrow the network. While you're regrowing the network in the hope of taking down the bad large network, other people have the same idea, and they start their own replacement networks and have to start from scratch themselves. Thus – and this, too, is necessary – you have simultaneously existing small networks that, taken together, have enough strength to topple the large network. They can only succeed because they're many. No individual small network takes down the big one on its own. You really don't topple the big guy until you have enough additive strength. But therein lies the problem.

Because no individual small network has enough strength on its own, it becomes difficult for any small network to sustain itself as small. Networks operate with greater efficiency and efficacity when they're large. The existence of another network, even only slightly bigger, threatens any smaller network. Thus, the small networks start to combine forces. Democratic governance of combined small networks, each of whose governing structures remain intact, gets difficult, so subject positions of leadership are consolidated. This process of combining and consolidation continues, and you end up with a large network again. Maybe that large network stays good for a while, but at a certain point, because the subject positions of leadership have been consolidated, you have less democracy, and that's when things go bad again. So is there a way out of this seemingly endless cycle?

If you're even only sort of a Hegelian, then you'd be inclined to answer no. Basically, what I've just described fits Hegel's idea of the dialectic. And what's that? Say you have a thing; let's call it a *thesis*. The thesis is stable for a while, but then it eventually gets opposed. Let's call the opposition the *antithesis*. The thesis and the antithesis get into it, and both are mutually destroyed but in a way that preserves parts of each in a new synthesis. The synthesis becomes the new thesis, it eventually gets opposed by yet another antithesis, and so on forever. And this only makes sense, for its basic assertion is that you start with something and that something lasts as long as there's stability. Stability only goes away when there's something to destabilize it, and that destabilized state only goes away when it becomes stable. You can't move from stable to stable or unstable to unstable because neither of those options is really a change in the situation. That makes such perfect sense, and that's why we probably get convinced that there's no way out. I'm not certain that's right, though.

When we're speaking about organizational structures, fitting things into the ever-spiraling dialectic presumes an engine that actually makes it perpetual. That engine is the creation of subject positions of leadership within any particular organizational structure. Remove the necessity of leadership, and you don't preserve the engine for the next go-round.

And if you're even sort of a Marxist, who himself was only the sort of Hegelian that I am – which is sort of – then you know that for the go-round that you want to be the final one, the engine that you mustn't preserve is money. You've got to get rid of the money. You don't need leadership in the first place when there's no money. To get out of the spiral, you've got to do stuff for free. Rich capitalist Marxists aren't a thing, yo. C.R.E.A.M.

Dollar, dollar bill, y'all

Here's a letter from Walter Benjamin to Gerhard Scholem. It's dated 19 February 1925:

> But for the moment I must breathe the tepid air: that is why I came here, and immediately picked up the nicest flu and sniffles. It is still questionable whether I will be able to turn anything in to Schultz before he leaves; the typing has just now begun. In any case, I will present myself to him very soon. The situation is not unfavorable . . . some things are positioned to practical advantage.[1]

As of this moment, it seems as though Benjamin thinks everything is more or less okay. So far, so good. However, knowing what we know, I can't help but feel like the kid who covers his ears before the gunshot goes off in Hitchcock's *North by Northwest*. Recently, I've seen some things on social media regarding the pay-to-play culture that sadly pervades academe. We all know about predatory journals and such, but folks have been pointing out in postings that some people use conference networking in the wrong way, meaning to an unfair advantage. Such exploitations are undeniable, but it's also true that things being positioned to practical advantage aren't always what they seem. In-person conferences are indeed great for finding folks so we can share sensitive information with like-minded others. However, apart from being harmful to the environment – like I said – conferences can be expensive and often inaccessible.

I've recently come up with a way to make a free virtual conference that makes use of free online resources to collect, review, present, and archive submissions. Furthermore, these free resources allow for greater accessibility. I do think knowledge should be a public good, and I've thought this since I began thinking about issues regarding what we do as scholars. However, I'm sad to say that I've only figured out how to put on a free virtual conference just recently. I'm not sad to say, however, that I decided to launch it as soon as I got the database architecture that supports it to work. I'm writing this in late April 2020. Also, this book is due 1 May. Also, I've been sick in bed for a really long time, so long that my memory-foam mattress doesn't even know who it is anymore. I guess this is how epiphanies come about.

The plan is to give this new conference its first go in November 2020. I'm calling it the Virtual Conference of Qualitative Inquiry, or VCQI for short. Vicky, by the way, was the name of one of my favorite aunts. Personally, I've always liked conferences and professional associations whose acronyms spell out things if you pronounce them. Also, a certain subversive conference organizer, a graduate student at the time – and this was back in the day, and it wasn't me, really, it wasn't – designed a logo for a conference that was in the shape of what they thought the eye of Sauron might look like. That the eye sits atop Barad-dûr is just a nice coincidence, a gift from the universe ... but I don't mean to be a bore. Also, Jasmine says that I can never tell this story – and now she's wondering why I'm bringing her into this – so I'm not doing either.

Anyway, free conference. I'm hoping that it's better late than never. Sorry, y'all, that it took me almost 18 years to figure out how stuff actually works. Right now, I'm trying to figure out what to put on the about page of the VCQI website. Let's see where all this goes. The typing has just now begun. . . .

https://vcqi.org/about/

VCQI is a free virtual conference for qualitative researchers. It's intended to offer an alternative to in-person conferences that can be expensive, non-inclusive, and harmful to the environment. Because it's asynchronous, attendees can choose to attend as many presentations as they find interesting. No presentation gets stuck in a bad time slot or has to go up against other sessions, so no set of presentations gets unfairly privileged over any others. VCQI is committed to the principle of minimal exclusivity and seeks to foster the sharing of knowledge to help make a better world.

VCQI is designed to be self-organizing and self-governing. It has no director, nor does it have other positions that reproduce hierarchical relations of power. Furthermore, there is no treasury. Being a free conference, it collects no submission fees. It seeks only to create partnerships, and it accepts no paid sponsorships. No one owns this conference, for it belongs, rather, to the community of people who'd like to participate.

Submissions

The submissions process is designed so that submitters have complete control over their content (more on that later). Furthermore, submissions are of completed video content only, not proposals. This ensures that the review process will remain fair regarding the already-carefully prepared presentations.

Submitters are asked to record a video or audio presentation prepared for the purpose of presenting at the VCQI conference and to post it on their own

YouTube channel before the submission closing dates of the conference. Content mustn't be in violation of YouTube's terms of service. To make the submissions accessible, at the time of posting, submitters are responsible for providing accurate closed captioning. If the presentation is in a language other than English, the video should provide English subtitles or a link to an English transcription.

Submissions are made through a Google Form linked to on the Submissions page. There are no submission or registration costs. To partake in VCQI is absolutely free. In order to submit, submitters are only asked to review two presentations in the area to which they make their submission.

On the submission form, submitters are asked to provide a URL to their recorded content. This content will be reviewed by two subsequent submitters. There's a limit of one submission per submitter per content area so that submitters cannot review their own submissions. The first two and last two submitters to a particular content area will receive reviews from separate members of the VCQI review committee.

Submitters retain the ability to control how their content is consumed. For instance, submitters may choose to enable or disable commenting, make the content public or unlisted, provide a link to the related paper in a repository, delete their postings if they so choose, and so on. The conference only asks that accepted submissions be left up for the duration of the conference for which the submission is accepted.

VCQI makes no claims to ownership of submitted content, accepted or otherwise. VCQI simply posts links to the content accepted in a conference program and publishes abstracts in proceedings should the submitter have opted in at the time of submission. At most, submitters will be invited for publication opportunities in nonpredatory, peer-reviewed publications. VCQI seeks to be a space where participants can promote the good work that they do.

Review process

Each submission will be made available to at least two reviewers who submit to the same content area for review. These two reviewers will make one of three recommendations: (1) Accept, (2) Resubmit, or (3) Reject. Reviewers will be asked to provide anonymous comments, a requirement if the decision is either Resubmit or Reject. Once these reviews are collected, acceptance to the final program of the conference will be decided as follows:

Two votes of Accept: Accepted for the conference.
Two votes of Resubmit: Invited to resubmit for the next conference.

Two votes of Reject: Rejected for the conference.
In the case of nonmatching votes, decisions will be made by the VCQI review committee.

Acceptance emails will be sent to the submitters after a final abstract review from the VCQI review committee, a review meant to ensure that no content includes (1) deliberate misinformation or unethically conducted research, (2) anything that can be deemed as "hate speech" broadly defined, or (3) any content that is in violation of YouTube's terms of service. Content containing anything from those three categories will be rejected. Furthermore, the VCQI review committee will review the reviews themselves so that no inappropriate content or trolling reviews will be passed on to submitters.

The conference

The conference program will be posted online on the vcqi.org site, listing the links to all accepted submissions. For those who've opted in at the time of submission, VCQI will make available proceedings containing the abstracts of accepted presentations.

VCQI reserves the right to remove from the conference program or proceedings any content found to contain (1) deliberate misinformation or unethically conducted research, (2) anything that can be deemed as "hate speech" broadly defined, or (3) any content that is in violation of YouTube's terms of service. If content is reported to be inaccessible, the submitters will be contacted and asked to make the content accessible. Failure to comply by the given deadline will result in removal from the program and/or proceedings.

Publication opportunities

VCQI seeks to establish and maintain relationships with publishers and editors of nonpredatory, peer-reviewed publication venues. These relationships are partnerships. VCQI will accept no paid sponsorships. This ensures that the partnerships serve our community. Our partnerships are designed to open publication opportunities for VCQI participants. For instance, prior to the conference itself, partnered journal editors will have exclusive first-look access to preliminary versions of the conference program. Partnered editors may then look for papers or panels that they could possibly invite for article submissions or special issues. Publisher partners are encouraged to look through conference content in order to find authors with whom they may cultivate relationships.

At the bottom, not ever wanting to prematurely punctuate any good discourse, VCQI seeks to be a venue where scholarly conversations might begin and continue throughout our social networks, both virtual and beyond.

Note

1 Benjamin, *The Correspondence of Walter Benjamin, 1910–1940*, 261.

4 Online media, social or otherwise

To post in a tweet...

Not only did Walter Benjamin have a radio show, but he also had some interesting thoughts on how radio would become our future in the past. In "Reflections on Radio," Benjamin laments that radio hasn't made full use of its potential to put as many people as possible "before the microphone at any opportunity, making the public witness to interviews and conversations in which anyone might have a say."[1] He didn't know it, but that's kind of what social media is in terms of its broadcast capabilities. Sticking more closely to radio, it's also really easy to do podcasts. Beyond something like radio, anyone with a smartphone has what can be used as a surprisingly good video camera, one with a much higher resolution and frame rate than what passed for broadcast television in the days of videotape. And if you have a decent video camera, you pretty much have your own free TV channel for which to schedule programming: because of the Internet.

For my part, I'll add to Benjamin's sentiments, and I'll say that we still haven't made full use of our current communication technology's potential to put as much scholarship out there when we feel inclined to produce it. Broadly speaking, any recorded content that we produce is a form of writing. When the publication and distribution of recorded communication were costly, not everyone could have a mic, so to speak. However, with those barriers mostly gone, why is it that our scholarly dissemination practices haven't caught up? Why, for instance, are we so caught up with publishing journal articles as though (1) that were our only option to put our writing out there and (2) that the only writing that counts as scholarship is words written on an actual page, either paper or digital?

As we're compelled to move our classes online, I think we'll see a change in the kind of recorded scholarship that gets counted for scholarly productivity. Already, altmetrics measure social media impact, and it's not difficult to imagine that at some point, having published in a high-impact-factor journal will be counted as roughly equivalent to having many recommendations or followers on something like ResearchGate. If we can't change the fact that the university will want to put metrics on us, I wouldn't see this change as a bad thing. If anything, recommendations and followers would be a more accurate metric because they at least imply a positive valence. Who knows what high citation counts really mean? What if your work is often cited as something not to do? It's occurred to me that publishing a deliberately horrible piece in a place where you could fly under the radar might be a way to troll those who, judging only by the numbers, fail to actually read the work in your portfolio.

So here, getting something actually published wouldn't be necessary if we started posting completed yet unpublished works in repositories. That's a practice easy enough to change. Post-publication peer review isn't so useful, but repositories do keep track of readership and whether readers find our work good. If you have 100 recommendations out of 120 readers, wouldn't we say that we have a better sample size than one consisting of two peer reviewers and an editor? But still, this is to go nowhere beyond words on a page.

... what everyone else says in a book

In its early days, narrative cinema took the form of filmed plays. The best seat in the house would be front and center, so that's where they put the camera, and it never moved. I feel that maybe this is where we are in terms of using media other than print when it comes to scholarship. With regard to several media, we haven't yet learned to write for the medium, so to speak. For instance, a lot of the nonprint scholarly media that one finds consists but of filmed lectures or PowerPoints with a voice-over. I guess what these have going for them is the fast-forward button.

I'm not saying that we need to be explosive, that we need to be a 30-second ad for salty snacks from the early to mid-1990s. There's nothing less cool than when one has to try. I learned that in high school from the ethnographic observations I conducted at the mall, for I, too, have seen it all – hi, Laurel Richardson! What I am saying, though, is that we might step up our game a bit. Why, for instance, are Laurel Richardson and Carolyn Ellis such good writers? It's because they spent a lot of time honing their craft, creating the conventions anew for a genre that they pioneered. And like Richardson and Ellis, one doesn't need to start from scratch. One can borrow from what's already out there.

If students don't typically find straight-up lectures engaging but prefer more interactive engagement in the classroom, why not try to approximate the latter in a recorded video? One could, for instance, record dialogue, rather than a soliloquy. Interviews are much more interesting to watch.

One might say, but why not, then, take this a step further and use teleconferencing? Maybe, but I don't think that's medium appropriate if many, many people are involved. For instance, every time someone opens a bag of Cheetos – speaking of salty snacks – the camera switches to them. Sure, you can mute everyone, but again, this is to film a play and not take advantage of the particular medium. Maybe teleconferencing is best when it's between three or four people.

Furthermore, maybe plentiful but short media is the way to go these days. When I used to teach cinema – a thing I did until very recently – I used to tease my students: Every semester I'd assign them a Tarkovsky film. If you haven't seen any, they're long. Watch this or that Tarkovsky film, I'd say, then I'd give them the runtime. After allowing for some collective moaning, I'd say, "Hey, three hours is short; I know y'all watch like eight 13-hour films back-to-back and then are sad when there isn't more. I believe you call it binge-watching." Different from Netflix and chill. Anyway, cut it up. Six to fifteen minutes seems to be the sweet spot.

And as for social media, maybe we've mastered the art of the repost, but this isn't exactly writing but citing. Maybe instead of partaking in social media fights or tweeting to complain, we might use the medium like a lovely scholarly journal that surprisingly still exists, seeing that it started in 1849. It's called *Notes and Queries*. Look it up if you don't know it. It's fascinating. If Nietzsche was the first to master the tweet, then *Notes and Queries* is Facebook and Reddit if they came in exquisitely bound volumes. Actually, if we're still keen to create new traditionally – but digitally – published journals, given how we've been producing and consuming social media text, I'm not sure that we shouldn't have more publications like *Notes and Queries*. Again, go plentiful but short. Easier to maintain content streams. Matches the market. Most important of all, having a place to publish short pieces and replies in a timely fashion better approaches the model of scholarly conversation. What genuine conversation takes several years to make only one round of exchange? The typical time to publication in traditional journals makes articles more like messages in a bottle than turns of dialogue. Now editing such a journal would be a herculean task, but there's a way to build an editor-less journal . . . more on that in the next chapter.

What everyone else does not say in a book

This is from Lacan's television address as recorded in *Television: A Challenge to the Psychoanalytic Establishment*:

> I always speak the truth. Not the whole truth, because there's no way, to say it all. Saying it all is literally impossible: words fail. Yet it's through

this very impossibility that the truth holds onto the real. I will confess then to having tried to respond to the present comedy and it was good only for the wastebasket. A failure then, but thereby, actually, a success when compared with an error, or to put it better: with an aberration. And without too much importance, since limited to this occasion. But first of all, which? The aberration consists in this idea of speaking so as to be understood by idiots. An idea that is ordinarily so foreign to me that it could only have been suggested to me. Through friendship. Beware. For there's no difference between television and the public before whom I've spoken for a long time now, a public known as my seminar. A single gaze in both cases: a gaze to which, in neither case, do I address myself, but in the name of which I speak.[2]

Maybe only someone with Lacan's sense of humor can try to pass this opening move off as a foray into what we know today as public scholarship. I'm not entirely certain that even he pulled it off. There's a point here, however.

In a publicly accessible medium, does it necessarily need to be the case that we address the public? Now, by asking this question, I'm not trying to set up an argument for elitism. Communicating in ways that are accessible to the greatest amount of charitable audience members is a good thing. Please choose to do so. However, we should remember that the public is a larger set than the one consisting of a charitable audience. Something that one puts on YouTube, for instance, can be viewed by anyone, and that includes folks who'd work against, let's say, a social justice agenda. And if we're sharing our strategies to fight oppression with those who might join us, isn't it better to keep those things a secret between the like-minded? If anything, by going public, don't we just weaken ourselves by opening ourselves up to being decontextualized and trolled?

The short answer to the last two questions is yes. It would be better to keep our strategies away from those who would oppress us, better to not be trolled. But this is a would-be *particular* better in the way that the better would be the ideal scenario. We don't, however, always have ideal scenarios as options open to us in the context of trying to pursue a *larger* better, in other words, a greater good.

The truth is out there. It always speaks. The truth can never really be a secret, for the truth is what's, at the end of the day, publicly available. If we're in the business of disclosing the truth, then all we really do is make the truth more accessible to those who are receptive. That the public may be populated, at least in part, by the deniers of truth is always a thing. We really can't let that deter us, though, trolls be damned. Sharing the truth when we discover it is the greater good that ought to be served. Otherwise, the oppressors win with very little work. That happens when we self-censor out of fear. Again, share fearlessly. Either way, the televisual gaze is one way. Speak from it; let the truth speak in the name of your *I*, and then hope for the best. That, and maybe go on the offense regarding the folks Lacan isn't speaking to. You can always turn off the comments.

Epistolary novel with friends

Here's another one from Benjamin's letters. The letter is dated 6 April 1925:

> This professor Schultz, who is insignificant in the world of scholarship, is a shrewd cosmopolitan who probably has a better nose for some literary matters than young coffee house habitués. But I have exhausted all there is to say about him with this blurb on his pseudo-intellectual cultural pretensions. He is mediocre in every other respect, and what he does have in the way of diplomatic skill is paralyzed by a cowardliness clothed in punctilious formality. I still have not heard anything about how my work has been received, or more precisely, anything good.[3]

Jasmine and I wondered about this, and we still sometimes do when we remember it: Before we really knew each other, both she and I had wanted to write the other one. Jasmine had wanted to thank me for what she had thought was my fine yet unrecognized academic labor. I later joked with her, asking did she mean *fine* on a scale of excellent, good, fine, poor? There's always truth in jokes, and I'm not sure if that really isn't how I'd rate what I've done over the years. . . . And I, on the other hand, wanted to write her about an article of hers that I really liked. We both wrote but let the email sit in the drafts folder for ages, hesitating because we were afraid of looking weird, as we both put it.

If you think about it, I'm sure this is at least somewhat relatable. One might have the urge to praise someone, but we often don't because what might the other person think of us? But that question in itself is a strange one, strange given the fact that we have no qualms about doing the opposite. How do I mean? We have reservations about praising someone in private, but we're all too quick to excoriate in public. We've all seen people try to embarrass others publicly at conferences, in lit reviews, and, now that social media is a thing, in social media especially. And I'm not talking about calling out bigoted people. That's one thing, a good thing. No, I'm talking about minor things that are otherwise meaningless: "Yes, yes, but you're working from assumptions made by early Derrida. How can you not acknowledge the shift in his thinking post *Specters of Marx*?" That's a real spoken sentence, by the way, only the minutiae were far more minute, and I've thus forgotten what the shift in thinking was, exactly. And it wasn't his turn to the political, which is big, but some obscure Hegel thing, if memory serves, that was different in *Glas*. At any rate, if one really wants to geek out about Hegel, that's fine, too, but it's especially cringe-worthy when one isn't aware of how petty this can be when not done in the friendly spirit of "let's argue over philosophy like how people at Comic-Con debate about the retconning in the new *Star Wars*." If any would-be intellectual deserves the prefix *pseudo–*, then it's the mediocre scholars who use big philosophical words only to bully: That's how Big *Pharmakon* gets you! I mean, sure, this sort of pettiness has become formalized in the scholarly discourse, but even though there's an etiquette for tearing people up, that doesn't make it any less cowardly.

The next time you download something you like – probably not quite legally posted – from a repository – your university library lacking a subscription – maybe send the person a nice note: not for flouting a transfer of copyright agreement but to congratulate them on work well done. Many of their citations might be in the context of being a surname in a string of surnames representing failures to address gaps in the literature. Thus, they're probably as insecure about the quality of their own work as we all tend to be. Impostor syndrome doesn't typically go away. Again, a nice thank you really shouldn't be all that weird, not when you think about it. It isn't, after all, antisocial media, even though it sometimes is. Also, who knows? You might make a friend, at least a pen pal.

The Qualitative Corner

This is the name of the YouTube channel Jasmine and I have. Its name is a deliberate acknowledgment of its modest ambitions. The channel is one that intends to help qualitative scholars promote the good work that they do, while also being a pedagogical resource. We'll review the work of qualitative scholars, have qualitative folks as guests for interviews, and do other sorts of things that, for now, go under the heading "*and more!*" I think as scholars, we ought to build our presence in media other than publications. And those non-publication media needn't always be textual only. There are several media which we've yet to fully explore. And though we qualitative folk might be comfortable where we are, there's much to be said for going beyond our little corner. I hope that we do.

Notes

1 Benjamin, "Reflections on Radio," 363.
2 Lacan, *Television: A Challenge to the Psychoanalytic Establishment*, 3.
3 Benjamin, *The Correspondence of Walter Benjamin, 1910–1940*, 263.

5 Reviewing

Stop, collaborate, and listen

Agamben tells a story of how he informed Derrida of a philological finding that makes the assertion traditionally attributed to Aristotle, "O friends, there are no friends," much less enigmatic. After some library research, Agamben found that in 1616, a correction of a diacritical mark and the addition of letter would make the translation read something to the effect of "He who has (many) friends, does not have a single friend."[1] Apparently, Agamben had brought this to Derrida's attention as he was preparing the lectures that later became the book *Politics of Friendship*, which takes "O friends, there are no friends" as its leitmotif. It thus surprised Agamben to see no mention of the alternate version when the book was published.

Is this a not so subtle dig against Derrida? Even though Agamben softens the critique, saying that perhaps there's something discomforting about the peculiar semantic status of the term *friend* for modern philosophers, one can certainly read it this way. I read it this way. I read it as "Derrida, why'd you publish a whole book on what's likely been a mistake reproduced for centuries when I showed you people had just been reading it literally incorrectly? It's clever, but it's wrong." I don't fault Agamben for writing this. Sometimes we try to be friends to people, but there comes a point. . . . Still, Agamben must've read the *Politics of Friendship* to have made the assessment that his suggestion went unacknowledged. Long story short: The truth of any text is missed when our disposition is to seek error. Charitable readings all around. There's a lot of insight in the *Politics of Friendship*, for instance, that we shouldn't just dismiss over a missing diacritical mark. Still, maybe listen to those collaborators who are our friendly readers.

Peer review

A well-known habit of good writing is to write with one's audience in mind. I'd add that it can't be good writing if the audience one has in mind is coterminous with all of humanity. Maybe you can please everyone, but in order to do so, you can't really take very many risks. Good writing communicates what an author thinks is important, and sometimes, what one thinks is important goes against the grain of at least large numbers of people. Such is the case when we take a small fraction of several billion. Take the first feminist scholars, for example. In its early days, feminist scholarship went against the grain, but feminists boldly asserted what needed to be asserted. Eventually, the courage of taking the risk to say what was important began to shape the discourse, opening areas wherein we could begin to address other issues of justice beyond the scope of feminism. By taking risks, feminist scholarship opened paths. In general, in the case of writing that promotes justice, risk-taking is both good and necessary, and it can't be the case that the author seeks to please the stubbornly bigoted among its audience. But making such claims about justice writing is safe territory. Here's a question that's less so: If it's true that good writing takes risks, is it possible to write well if one writes something that will be peer-reviewed?

From within the way we practice reviewing for publication in the interpretive social sciences and much of the humanities, risk-taking is profoundly discouraged by the structure of the institution of review itself. As an early-career scholar, if the stakes of getting a manuscript accepted are whether or not I keep my job, it seems that the most rational choice when it comes to my own interests is to play it safe. Thus, apart from the reviewing editor, I write to please a potential peer reviewer. I have no idea who this peer reviewer will be. And because the peer reviewer might be anyone, I must write for everyone. In other words, if I want my manuscript to be published, I write for an audience of one who isn't anyone in particular. Writing for someone but no one in particular is tantamount to writing for an audience that's coextensive with all of humanity, something that one can't do if one is to write well. True, in practice, I might not have to write for all of humanity when I try to produce a manuscript, but with regard to some disciplines, the distribution of disagreement within the particular discipline may come close to modeling the distribution we'd expect to find among literally everyone anyway. Given that it's a topic that several people have constructed arguments about, in the bodies of literature making up our respective disciplines, aren't we likely to find a near exhaustion of the possibilities: Someone or other says such and such a position is absolutely right, another that says it's absolutely wrong, and many others argue that it's actually somewhere in between?

Of course, this applies to peer review in areas of scholarship where peer review doesn't mean that someone can try to reproduce our results. In the sciences wherein reproducibility can be held as the standard by which we value importance, we have it easy. Either someone else can observe neutrinos traveling faster than light or they can't. If they can't, then that suggests that something was wrong with the initial observation. There's peer review in the traditional sense, but now there's also such a thing as post-publication peer review, let alone the mess of quick-to-anger scholars on social media, altmetrics, and trolls from every place imaginable, all of which are a sort of peer review unto themselves, sort of, but perhaps are now the most influential.

O, were it only the case that we'd not take up peer review as an opportunity to kill ideas we don't like or even help people write a better article. The latter may be well intentioned, but if this better isn't limited to truer, that presumes that the reviewer is a better writer to begin with, and such a presuming is presumptuous, for this *better* would be but a matter of taste. Further still, peer review should definitely not be a mechanism by which to scoop people on ideas by rejecting their work only to repackage and steal it. This is the most reprehensible type of plagiarism.

Ideally, if we want something that really sticks closely to the conversational, peer review should be limited to deciding whether a manuscript is making an internally coherent contribution to the conversation. In other words, the only question that any peer reviewer should answer is, Do all the elements of this manuscript contribute to an argument that rational thought might consider as being true? *Rational* is the important part here. Things like bigoted thought, of course, aren't rational. At bottom, however, whether knowingly or not, good intentions or no, going any further beyond the only question of peer review devolves into censorship. As it stands, peer review is too disposed to seeking only what's wrong with a text and rejecting it on that basis. We might instead orient ourselves to finding what's right and cultivating that in generative ways. Alas, we might hope for a broad change someday, but we need to do something in the meantime.

Too close to see

I'm not making the argument that our review practices are a bad idea in general. Like many things, it's a wonderful idea if we adhere to just principles that inform the practice. I suppose that I'm a bit of a proceduralist in this sense. I am saying, however, that reviewing practices can be very bad when we forget to have just principles in the first place. So if it's a good thing to have friends read our work so that we can be part of actual conversations – and this is the good we can pursue in the meantime of waiting for peer-review practices to change in such a way where it doesn't cause us anxiety as writers – let's now take a moment to think about how to make peer review a good thing consistently. We sometimes get it right, but perhaps we can make a procedure out of when we do. Let's continue on the path of thinking through this Agamben and Derrida thing, for an answer lies in further exploration. It involves the occluded perception of the friend and the intimacy only afforded to strangers.

Before the passage earlier, earlier from where Agamben digs into Derrida at least a little, and after a bit of a preface, Agamben opens his essay by telling a story about how he and his friend Jean-Luc Nancy decided to exchange some letters on the idea of friendship. It was an exchange of only two letters in total. In Agamben's words,

> [t]his is not the place to attempt to comprehend what reasons – or, perhaps, what misunderstandings – signaled the end of the project upon the arrival of Jean-Luc's letter. But it is certain that our friendship – which we assumed would open up a privileged point of access to the problem – was instead an obstacle, and that it was, in some measure, at least temporarily, obscured.[2]

It isn't difficult to see why discussing the idea of friendship with a friend would be an obstacle. Now that I'm getting a little older and the fact that I've needed reading glasses for quite some time is getting more and more difficult to disavow, I know that there are times when you're too close to see the thing you're closest to. This must work figuratively, too. In fact, Agamben makes the same observation a few pages later when he discusses a painting by Giovanni Serodine depicting the meeting of the apostles Peter and Paul. Agamben says that the two are painted in such close proximity, their foreheads nearly stuck together, that they couldn't possibly see each other from that distance, and this was, to him, the perfect allegory of friendship.[3] It makes sense, then, why it would be nearly impossible to explore the idea of friendship with a friend.

Might it not also be the case that we might be asking too much of a friend to read our work in all the ways it needs to be read? If we can expect some myopia from noncharitable readers, might we not also expect some presbyopia from our friends? Being close might help with giving charitable readings, but at this distance, some things might be but a blur. This is to say that there's something to be said for not only the perspective available to the stranger but maybe also the perspectives of many of them.

Under pressure

Here's another Benjamin letter, a letter dated 20–25 May 1925:

> Another factor is Schultz's unreliability. He naturally does not want to reveal his weak point to me. Thus he let drop a few short, forced words of great appreciation for my habilitation dissertation, but does not want to put himself out. Thus at the moment there is no one who can say what will come of it. I am able to identify a number of benevolently

neutral gentlemen on the faculty, but I do not know anyone who would actually take up my cause.[4]

It's too much to ask an author to identify who may take up their cause, especially when those people decide whether you continue in the discipline or you don't. How might we fix this?

Let's think about reviews of products on commercial websites. I often find the reviews to be helpful, and what helps me decide whether I trust a review is that I can look at the profile of the reviewer themselves and I can see how many others have found a particular review helpful. Sometimes, the reviews are even in dialogue with each other. There's a way we can use this model for peer review for digital journals, provided that we set up the journal's architecture in a certain way. Namely, we need to have a publicly available prepublication repository at the front end.

Journals get in trouble because they find it difficult to find anyone to agree to peer review. I think we ought to be good citizens, because publication doesn't happen without review, but reviews don't have the recognition of publications, so this is perhaps why people are reluctant to do them. So maybe there's a way to incentivize reviewers. Creating a currency such as publons might eventually be a solution, but it's too indirect. You get into all kinds of exchange value trouble, and this a part of capitalism that isn't worth reproducing. Rather, I think we could structure a journal such that in order to make a submission, one needs to have done a certain number of non-anonymous reviews for the journal that are ranked as helpful by other reviewers. The reviews need to be non-anonymous to prevent trolling. The reviews need to be ranked as helpful to a certain threshold to ensure one carefully crafts honest reviews. And the requirement of reviewing in the first place is a good faith showing that one cares to participate in the community of researchers gathered by the journal. And for this to happen, a necessary component of this journal is that its submissions be in an open digital repository. This repository should give a DOI number to submissions to prevent others from stealing work and so that the works may be cited should someone choose to do so prior to official publication.

Regarding these reviews, depending on how a particular author of a submission opts in, they can choose to make public certain or all reviews or to keep them totally private. They can use any review feedback that they get to make revisions as they so choose. Furthermore, because submitting to the journal isn't an official submission to an editor to have the manuscript reviewed, only a making publicly available one's own work, authors are free to simultaneously attempt to publish in a more traditional journal. Submission to the prepublication repository doesn't necessarily entail that the manuscript is under review, for reviewers are not invited but volunteer.

To set up this architecture as self-sustaining, one would only initially need an editorial team of fair reviewers following the principle of doorpersoning. In other words, let in everyone who may have business inside, and because the journal would be digital, there wouldn't be issues of capacity. Lacking community reviewers at first, the initial team of reviewers would make available an initial batch of submissions. Once there are enough community reviewers, input from the journal's editorial team may become unnecessary, and the journal becomes self-sustaining from the perspective of review.

This kind of setup solves the problem of making accessible unpublished but important content. Null results not being published, for instance, are a good example of such content. If null results aren't published, then people waste time repeating a study because they're unaware that anyone did such a study. They're unaware because the write-up only exists as an archived rejected manuscript in a submission system somewhere or on someone's laptop. Really, having access to unpublished works are good for the whole of the community. In general, we can see what works and what doesn't. We don't have to wonder if good ideas were gatekept. Ideas that are ahead of their time aren't rejected, but if they aren't withdrawn by the author, they are simply as yet to be accepted. Why should only editors have this sort of access to the unpublished?

And in this new kind of journal, what of publication itself? A threshold of total positive reviews against negative reviews can be determined depending upon the size of the community. Any article passing this threshold is invited for publication. Should the author accept, then the article is copyedited, a transfer of copyrights is issued, the article is slotted for an official publication date, and so on.

And as for whether such articles will count toward renewal or promotion? I think that a strong case can be made to universities to count such articles because they're actually more robustly peer-reviewed than most traditional journals with high impact factors. At most, peer review is traditionally only a small sample size of the community, granted that the editor could find reviewers at all. Judgments can be made by the size of the journal's reviewing community, the number of positive reviews, the number of reads, and other such transparent metrics. These metrics would be more immediate than waiting on an article to receive citations. For instance, we all know that there are a number of widely read and influential articles that people steal from because they deliberately choose not to cite to pass off the good ideas as their own. Citation counts aren't valenced as positive or negative, and impact factors are too easy to unfairly influence.

The only obstacle I see to starting such a journal is a certain few bad-actor editors who enjoy their positions as gatekeepers but who are otherwise unreliable when it comes to serving their community of researchers. For instance, I have it on good word from a number of well-respected scholars that a certain editor intentionally publishes the worst material received from methodological perspectives that they dislike. This is for the purpose of creating a long-term straw-man argument to support the things that they do like. Suffice to say, editors such as this one in particular might not want to put themselves out because their positions of power are comfortable, and they're easily threatened by the larger research community who's been on the verge of realizing what they've been up to. This isn't to say that all editors are bad, of course. On the contrary, most of the editors I know are very good and seek to serve their community in the best ways they can. I have the urge to list them all, but then that would leave out good folks that I don't know. It's only the case that there are a handful of bad ones, but their reputation is already known in their research communities, known such that this is, I'm sure, news to very few. Editors such as these don't serve the community or the publishers who initially trusted them. Removing people you installed in good faith gets difficult because too late comes all too fast, all too often.

And as for the willingness of publishers to take a risk on doing something like this? I do understand that going all in on a project like the one outlined here could be an expensive failure. That's why I suggest hacking things like ResearchGate to do what I described above so that we can give a brave publisher a proof of concept. If people don't want to hack ResearchGate, then the Virtual Conference of Qualitative Inquiry could possibly serve as a proof of concept to a certain extent, albeit in a different medium. Can you tell that I just really badly want for something like this to exist? Anyway, at the end of the day, if you believe that this sort of thing can work, then let's please try to get this going! We can start by spreading the word.

Thesis IX and "Angelus Novus"

Here's something from Benjamin's *The Arcades Project*:

> Perhaps the most deeply hidden motive of the person who collects can be described this way: he takes up the struggle against dispersion. Right from the start, the great collector is struck by the confusion, by the scatter, in which the things of the world are found.[5]

I'm not against the idea of editors in general. I do think that editors shouldn't be bad, self-serving actors, but good editors can do a lot of good. However, it occurs to me that if we build from a particularly configured architecture, we could broaden the horizons regarding how things get gathered under the title of a journal. Collections typically belong to a collector, but then this reflects the tastes only of the collector. Ideally, if the community is good, it would be better that the tastes of the community be reflected rather than those of only one or a few members of that community. While it isn't a bad thing to have such collections serving narrow tastes, it would be a good thing to create collections that serve broader tastes also. Both can exist alongside each other.

I believe that the architecture for a journal outlined in the preceding section doesn't necessarily need an editor. The large sample peer review is really all that's necessary. All you'd need is a database, and perhaps a database administrator, to send invitations to authors who go beyond a certain threshold of recommendations. I think an editor-less journal – or one that uses crowdsourced editing – might be a useful thing to explore. First, consumers of the journal's content can have something curated from what would otherwise be the confusion of dispersion and have the thing remedying the scatter not be the tastes of one or a few. But equally important, I think this allows publishers – with whom authors live in a necessary symbiosis – to not have to pay large percentages of royalties to editors or give other support money. Instead, these savings could be passed on to libraries that are already trying to resist journal subscription bundles. This resistance from librarians is understandable, but then this threatens the symbiosis. I think what I'm describing might serve as a good compromise; it could at least be the opening to such a conversation.

"Ah, if only we could start such a journal . . ." he trailed off longingly, as though addressing no one in particular.

Notes

1 Agamben, *What Is an Apparatus? And Other Essays*, 27.
2 Ibid., 26.
3 Ibid., 30–31.
4 Benjamin, *The Correspondence of Walter Benjamin, 1910–1940*, 266.
5 Benjamin, *The Arcades Project*, 211.

6   Teaching

This old future, *current* and *final*?

Here's something from a lecture collected in Nietzsche's *On the Future of Our Educational Institutions*:

> The purpose of education, according to this scheme, would be to rear the most "current" men possible, – "current" being used here in the sense in which it is applied to the coins of the realm. The greater the number of such men, the happier a nation will be; and this precisely is the purpose of our modern educational institutions: to help every one, as far as his nature will allow, to become "current"; to develop him so that his particular degree of knowledge and science may yield him the greatest possible amount of happiness and pecuniary gain.[1]

In Nietzsche's critique of what seemed to be a dismal future for education, we can see that the neoliberal tendency of how universities approach education – framed here as a scheme not to follow – isn't so *neo–* as we may sometimes like to think. I'm reminded of another passage that comes from a talk Jean-Luc Nancy gave, transcribed in *Being With the Without*:

> Recently I discovered what the word *finance* means. Its etymology comes from *final*, that is, to make an end in some action or operation. And the end is to pay. I pay you, or you pay me, so that the whole relationship is finished. . . . Thus, financial capitalism is extreme capitalism not because, as one often hears today, it is some kind of excess of capitalism. The idea is that today's capitalism is "too much," and that we have to control it and return to "good" capitalism. But there is no good capitalism, for many reasons, but also because capitalism represents the whole extent of the "non-co," the non-sensibility of togetherness,

and the replacement of togetherness, of the "co," by Marx' "general equivalence," money.[2]

So the coins of currency and the finality of financial capitalism: When you boil it down, under capitalism, money is what's now and what puts an end to a way of how we relate to one another. Once we're all paid up, there's no reason for the togetherness of being-with. This is how it was, and this is how it shall always be ended throughout the eternal, current present. At least this is what ideology would have us believe. Slavoj Žižek repeats this a lot, and according to Žižek, it seems to have been something that Frederic Jameson said, which is that it's easier to imagine the end of the world than it is to imagine the end of capitalism.

But if education becomes but another support for capitalism, we might not need to imagine the end of the world. We do, after all, live in the Anthropocene. I think this is a good reason to return to teaching as the most important function of the university. If there's anything that can undo the capitalist ideology that's gotten us to the place in which we find ourselves, it's teaching. We may get very little recognition for it, but it might be teaching that saves the world. And we might have to teach beyond the brick walls of our institutions.

Can I kick it?

My first thought was, "This can't be how I die, right?" My second thought was to climb. I was in the collapsing stacks at our library. Someone didn't see me and pushed the button to get to another set of shelves while I was still inside. I was in the middle, so running to either end might've taken too long. The shortest way was up. I got about two shelves high when it occurred to me that I might yell. Third thought's a charm. Whoever it was then pushed the emergency stop. When I got back downstairs to check out all my books, I told the librarian that someone almost crushed me in the stacks. She said, "That happens more often than you'd think, but there's an automatic kill switch, kind of like an elevator, so it's totally safe." I asked her where that switch was for future reference, and she told me that it really wasn't a switch, exactly. It was a kickplate. As I said, my second thought was to climb. My fourth thought retroactively became "I almost died in something like that one trash compactor scene in the only good *Star Wars* movie."

My own history repeated itself: first literally, then as a metaphor. I often feel overwhelmed by the crushing weight of the library, and as a scholar, I feel responsible for reading as much of it as I can. I don't suppose that this is rare. And yet, one of the things we value most is to add to the library.

We're better scholars if we publish a lot. But might we rethink this? Why isn't teaching what's most valued?

Discourse of the university

> What use has the university been? This can be read according to each epoch. By virtue of the increasingly extreme denudation of the master's discourse, the university discourse finds itself displaying – all the same, don't think it's shaken or finished – that for the moment it's encountering a heap of difficulties. These difficulties can be approached at the level of the close relationship that exists between the student's position of always being, in the university discourse, in a more or less masked manner, identified with this object *a*, which is charged with producing what? The barred S.[3]

This passage is from Lacan's *Seminar XVII*. Here, he's describing one discourse of four, the discourse of the university. In his theory of the four discourses, one can think of object *a* as a surplus and the barred S as the subject. So here, the university discourse puts the students in the position of being the surplus. The students, in other words – other Marxist words – are the exploited of the university, and they're charged with producing the subject. All of this is, we suppose, in the service of knowledge. And if we borrow from Lacan's colleague Althusser – but also from Nietzsche earlier – we know that education as an ideological state apparatus reproduces inequalities of wealth and power. Lacan's point is that the student is in the position of the exploited laborer. When they get out from under education, they're still under the yoke of a subjectivity that – and we can say this in a very literal way – makes them exploited laborers once they enter the job market.

Think, for a moment, about the career path for too many of our graduate students. We use graduate student labor for research and teaching purposes and – when acting in bad faith – assign them all the dirty work that we don't want to do. Bad faith actors take the credit for the work of their students, and perhaps assuage their own guilt by thinking that there's a vague promise that their students will someday be in a better, perhaps tenured, position. However, not only do the limited tenured spaces not open up; they're also rapidly vanishing. Thus, the system we have now creates several temporary, cheap-labor positions for work that the privileged don't want to do – positions putting too many students into great debt – makes promises of good, stable jobs that don't exist, and those jobs don't exist because we've swapped them out for positions no better than the temporary ones that were offered from the outset. Is this what we do in the name of pursuing knowledge? With regard to our graduate students whose primary aim is to learn, is this what we try to pass off as teaching? We promise "Hey, don't worry; we'll let you in!" But then, at the last possible moment, we yank it away.

And not to be heavy-handed, but Shultz and Benjamin: Who wants to be Benjamin in this position, but even more so, who wants to be a Shultz? The latter shouldn't be one's legacy. Still, it's never too late to change course.

Furthermore, if the university focuses only on STEM (science, technology, engineering, and mathematics), then I'm not sure that anything challenges this system of the university discourse. We do need the disciplines where they might encounter Lacan, Marx, Althusser, and Nietzsche, I'd say. We qualitative folks are sitting in a comparatively nice position with regard to folks in areas such as philosophy, history, and the literatures. I think we need to collaborate. Remember when I was talking about using Professor Facebook – the digital scholarly repositories with social media features – to find pen pals? Maybe reach out to some of our friends in the humanities. Let's prop each other up a bit. We qualitative folk might venture beyond our qualitative corner. In the moment, it seems necessary.

The ultimate pen

From a letter dated 21 July 1925:

> I immediately turned to Salomon for more precise information. He was unable to find out anything other than that it was generally thought advisable for me to withdraw my application as quickly as possible in order that I might be spared an official rejection. Schultz . . . had, of course, assured me he wanted to spare me that in any case. He remained incommunicado. I have very cogent reasons for assuming that he behaved in extremely bad faith. . . . It is quite unheard of that a project like mine could be authorized and then ignored in this way. Because – I remember this much of the penultimate stage of the process about which I must have written you – when all is said and done, it was Schultz, who, before the faculty, opposed my getting a degree in literary history and thus brought about the current situation[4]

We know that story of Benjamin's manuscript eventually ends in publication, but at this point in the story, he's in a difficult place. As my own book is here about to come to a close, I'm wondering where we are as scholars. I'd like the penultimate section to be a happy ending, with the ultimate section being a nice denouement. I think the most I can offer, however, is that things are uncertain, and we've much work ahead of us.

In general, when things start to shift into something different, it's almost always certain that the paths ahead will be filled with things not going our way, achievements that don't forestall inevitable losses, and immeasurably hard work to merely keep the ground we have, let alone the making of any progress. And here, perhaps we should avoid the temptation to use militant metaphors of war and perpetual struggle. While these might rouse us, and while Hegel's concept of *Aufhebung* is a useful one, we don't have to slide into the darker parts of his philosophy of history. Instead of a struggle for recognition in a fight to the death for pure prestige, I think it's more useful to see history itself as a but a series of events that are either successful or failed rejections. Historically speaking, we hope that we successfully reject the bad and hope that rejections of the good eventually fail. And still, even without any acceptance, rejected things of good can have value nonetheless inasmuch as the care of taking responsibility for disclosing truth is instrumentally valuable even should that aim never reach the final good. And so goes something similar for the things we should reject. Even should we, after a long journey, determine that we had been on a mistaken path, given that we were aimed toward the disclosure of truth to begin with, we at least now know which ways not to take.

At the end of the day, rejection isn't something we should always avoid altogether. Partly taking a cue from eudaimonism, I think that if we can keep the focus of our actions on the pursuit of the flourishing of all – and really, isn't this the reason behind the philosophical aim of disclosing truth? – we mustn't let fear of rejection steer us, for rejection is mostly what there is, and this itself mostly because – whether we like it or not – it can't be otherwise if even there remains even a little bit of truth to disclose. Put another way, what should steer us is trying to discover what closures of truth to reject, so we should thus take a more welcoming position regarding at least some types of rejection. And, that being said, because flourishing for all is important; as academics in pursuit of truth, we ourselves can't fail to recognize the importance of necessary but unrecognized work that's unpublished. And it really ought to occur to us that the important and necessary unrecognized work can go generally under the name of one's teaching.

My Teaching

This is from Lacan's *My Teaching*:

> That is always how it ends. When you have been dead long enough, you find yourself being summed up in three lines of a textbook – though where I am concerned, I'm not too sure which textbook it will be. I cannot foresee which textbooks I will figure in because I cannot foresee anything to do with the future of my teaching.[5]

It's in this way that Lacan begins his lecture "The Place, Origin and End of My Teaching," a lecture collected in *My Teaching*. I think this beginning is a nice ending for us here, for this ending is also a beginning for myself. In the past couple of years, my career has shifted somewhat. I've moved from teaching exclusively undergraduates to teaching graduate students, I just recently launched a virtual conference, Jasmine and I have already banked a few episodes of the first season of what I hope will be a long-running YouTube channel, and I now find myself in the position of being an editor of three different types of publications. I've used the opportunity to publish this book to reflect on guiding principles that I'd like to follow when serving on dissertation committees, in maintaining a conference format that's as inclusive and accessible as it can be, and in cultivating an online presence and to think through what principles I ought to follow in my capacity as an editor. As for teaching, my students have always kept me going. That's the one thing that hasn't changed. It's the part of my job that's most dear and enjoyable to me. I always have much love for my students.

Lacan's words about the future of his teaching, however, resonate with me. For him, it was a question concerning the future of psychoanalysis, but for me, it's the question concerning the Anthropocene.

The world we know needs help. Curtailing a mass extinction event isn't the most important issue among many, but for any living being for whom there's a future, it is itself the very precondition of pursuing justice, fairness, and flourishing. Second, so long as life remains, we must continue to make certain that the world is such that there is justice, fairness, and flourishing with regard to all living beings, both present and yet to come. Working together, we can make this happen.

Science, policy, and legislation will be needed to make it through the ongoing climate crisis as best as we can. Those of us who work in these areas must act urgently because preventing worst-case scenarios will take both time and maximal effort. Maximal effort isn't currently being put forth, and with every passing moment, we run shorter on time.

Those of us whose work involves justice, fairness, and flourishing but who work outside of the areas of science, policy, and legislation must continue to do the important work that we do. However, we must do our part – along with as many people as possible – to make time for those who work in the areas of science, policy, and legislation. How might we make this time? Here are some suggestions:

1 Personally determine the point beyond which consumption is excessive with regard to living a good life; then consume no more than that.
2 Come to an understanding of the point of consumption below which it's impossible to live a good life, and strictly adhering to the principle of

fairness, do everything you're able to make sure that no being capable of living a good life falls below its minimum.
3   Do all these things absolutely inclusively with regard to justice. Do this through a principle of minimal exclusivity, meaning that you only exclude things that are unfairly exclusive. Note that you can't adhere to the principle of minimal exclusivity if you exclude the beings capable of living a good life who are yet to come.
4   Widely disseminate ways that will give us more time to figure out how to move beyond the climate crisis both through education and through any communicative medium by which knowledge can be shared.

More on all this to come. Until then, take care of yourself and each other.

Notes

1 Nietzche, *On the Future of Our Educational Institutions*, 51.
2 Nancy, *Being With the Without*, 16–17.
3 Lacan, *Book XVII*, 148.
4 Benjamin, *The Correspondence of Walter Benjamin, 1910–1940*, 275–276.
5 Lacan, *My Teaching*, 3.

Works cited

Agamben, Giorgio. *What Is an Apparatus? And Other Essays*. 2006. Translated by David Kishik and Stefan Pedatella, Stanford UP, 2009.
Benjamin, Walter. *The Arcades Project*. 1982. Translated by Howard Eiland and Kevin McLaughlin, Harvard UP, 1999.
———. *The Correspondence of Walter Benjamin, 1910–1940*. Translated by Manfred R. Jacobson and Evelyn M. Jacobson, U of Chicago P, 1994.
———. "A Crazy Mixed-Up Day: Thirty Brainteasers." In Lecia Rosenthal, editor, *Radio Benjamin*. 6 July 1932. Translated by Jonathan Lutes, Lisa Harries Schumann, and Diana K. Reese, Verso, 2014, pp. 189–196.
———. *The Origin of German Tragic Drama*. 1963. Translated by John Osborne, Verso, 1998.
———. "Reflections on Radio." In Lecia Rosenthal, editor, *Radio Benjamin*. C. 1930–1931. Translated by Jonathan Lutes, Lisa Harries Schumann, and Diana K. Reese, Verso, 2014, pp. 363–364.
Burman, Erica. *Fanon, Education, Action: Child as Method*. Routledge, 2018.
Cage, John. *Silence: Lectures and Writings*. 1939–1958. Wesleyan UP, 2013.
Emerson, Ralph Waldo. "The American Scholar." *Phi Beta Kappa Society*, 1837, Harvard University, Cambridge. Lecture. In Digital Emerson: A Collective Archive, http://digitalemerson.wsulibs.wsu.edu/exhibits/show/text/the-american-scholar
Fuss, Diana. *Essentially Speaking: Feminism, Nature & Difference*. Routledge, 1989.
Germano, William. *From Dissertation to Book*. U of Chicago P, 2005.
Harney, Stefano, and Fred Moten. *The Undercommons: Fugitive Planning & Black Study*. Minor Compositions, 2013.
Hoenle, Sandra Vivian Bert. *Walter Benjamin: The Production of an Intellectual Figure*, PhD dissertation. University of British Columbia, 1999.
Kojève, Alexandre. *Introduction to the Reading of Hegel: Lectures on the Phenomenology of Spirit*. 1947. Translated by James H. Nichols, Jr., Cornell UP, 1980.
Lacan, Jacques. *My Teaching*. 2005. Translated by David Macey, Verso, 2008.
———. *The Seminar of Jacques Lacan: Book III: The Psychoses 1955–1956*. 1981. Translated by Russell Grigg, W. W. Norton & Co., 1997.
———. *The Seminar of Jacques Lacan: Book XVII: The Other Side of Psychoanalysis*. 1991. Translated by Russell Grigg, W. W. Norton & Co., 2007.

———. *Talking to Brick Walls: A Series of Presentations in the Chapel at Sainte-Anne Hospital.* 1971–1972. Translated by Adrian R. Price, Polity, 2017.

———. *Television: A Challenge to the Psychoanalytic Establishment.* 1974. Translated by Jeffrey Mehlman, W. W. Norton & Co., 1990.

Nancy, Jean-Luc. *Being with the Without.* Axl Books, 2013.

Nietzsche, Friedrich Wilhelm. *The Complete Works of Friedrich Nietzsche, Vol. 3: On the Future of Our Educational Institutions.* 1924. Translated by J. M. Kennedy, T. N. Foulis, 1910.

Singh, Julietta. *Unthinking Mastery: Dehumanism and Decolonial Engagements.* Duke UP, 2018.

Spivak, Gayatri Chakravorty. *The Spivak Reader: Selected Works of Gayati Chakravorty Spivak.* Routledge, 1995.

West, Cornel. *Keeping Faith: Philosophy and Race in America.* Routledge, 1993.

Index

accessibility 16, 23, 25–26, 39, 47
Agamben, Giorgio 11, 34, 36–37
Allen, Mitch ix
Althusser, Louis 44–45
Aristotle 34
Aufhebung 46

Benjamin, Walter 15, 45; *The Arcades Project* 40; "A Crazy Mixed-Up Day: Thirty Brainteasers" 5; letters 23, 32, 37–38; *The Origin of German Tragic Drama* 7–8; "Reflections on Radio" 28
Burman, Erica xi
Butler, Judith viii, ix, 11, 20–21

Cage, John xi, 2–3
capitalism 1, 14, 16, 23, 38, 42–43
climate crisis 47–48
collections 4, 40–41
conferences 17, 20–27, 32, 47; *see also* Virtual Conference of Qualitative Inquiry (VCQI)
consensus 16

Derrida, Jacques ix, 32, 34, 36
dialectic: large and small networks 21–23; lord and bondsman 13, 16
digital, the 4, 7–8, 30, 38–39, 45
disagreement 12, 16, 35
disciplines 6, 12, 20–21, 35, 45
discourse ix, 9, 13, 16, 33, 35, 44–45
dissertations 11–19
doorperson 4, 39

editors 3–4, 26, 38–41, 47
exclusivity 1, 24, 48

fairness 17, 47–48
Fanon, Frantz xi
Freire, Paolo xi
Fuss, Diana viii

gatekeeping 3–4, 39
Germano, William viii, ix, 11

Harney, Stefano x–xi
Hegel, Georg Wilhelm Friedrich ix–xi, 13–14, 16, 22, 33
Hoenle, Sandra Vivian Berta 15

inclusivity 47–48

Jameson, Frederic 43
justice 21, 31, 35, 47–48

Kojève, Alexandre xi, 14

Lacan, Jacques ix–xi; mirror stage essay 20; *My Teaching* 46–48; *Seminar III* 15–16; *Seminar XVII* 44; *Talking to Brick Walls* 9–10; television address 30–31
legislation 47
literature reviews 13

Marcuse, Herbert 14
Marxism viii, 14, 22–23, 44
methodology 5, 12, 16, 40
Metz, Christian 20
money 23–25, 41, 42–43
Moten, Fred x–xi
Mulvey, Laura 20

Index

Nancy, Jean-Luc 37, 42–43
networks 1, 13, 15, 21–23
Nietzsche, Friedrich Wilhelm 30, 42–45

online media 23, 28–33, 36, 45
Other, the 15–16

peer review 4, 29, 34–36, 38–39, 41
perspective 36–37
policy 47
positivism 9, 29, 39
pressure 9, 15, 37–40
principles 1, 24, 36, 39, 47–48
publishing 3–4, 6, 8–10, 25–30, 34–35, 38–41

qualitative, the 9, 12, 20, 33, 45; *see also* Virtual Conference of Qualitative Inquiry (VCQI)
Qualitative Corner, The 33
quantitative, the 12

recognition ix–xi, 14–19, 38, 43, 46
rejections 3–4, 7–9, 25–26, 36, 39, 45–46
ResearchGate 29, 40
review 3–4, 23–26, 34–41; *see also* peer review

Scholem, Gershom 7, 23
science 12, 42, 47
Shakespeare, Hannah ix
sharing 1–2, 21, 23–24, 31–32, 48
Singh, Julietta x–xi
social media *see* online media
Spivak, Gayatri Chakravorty ix–x
submissions 23–26, 38–39

teaching 9–10, 18, 42–48
tenure 3, 17, 44

universities 15–18, 39, 42–45
university discourse viii, xi, 1, 44–45

VCQI *see* Virtual Conference of Qualitative Inquiry (VCQI)
Virtual Conference of Qualitative Inquiry (VCQI) 23–27, 40
virtual conferences 47; *see also* Virtual Conference of Qualitative Inquiry (VCQI)

West, Cornel viii, x

YouTube 25–26, 31, 33, 47

Žižek, Slavoj x, 43